THE GENTLE ART OF
and other important things

THE GENTLE ART OF MATCHMAKING

and other important things

John B. Keane

THE MERCIER PRESS
CORK and DUBLIN

THE MERCIER PRESS,

4 Bridge Street, Cork

25 Lower Abbey Street, Dublin 1

First published 1973

Copyright © John B. Keane 1973

SBN 85342 326 1

Contents

The Gentle Art of Matchmaking 7
A Farewell to Salads 11
The China Half-Set 14
Compositions 18
Gambles 21
The Papers 24
Trotters 28
Socks 31
Spectacles 34
Periwinkles 38
The Ass and Cart 41
Ribbons 45
Bohareens 48
Butt-sucking 52
Morning Socials 55
Latch Keys 58
Great Goalkeepers of Our Time 61
Sideway Talkers 65
The Spirit of Christmas 69
Boasting 72
Paddling 76
Watery Eyes 79
The Mouse's Return 82
Noses 86
Knives 89
A Dear Neighbour 92
Good News 95
Cat-Calls 98
Skinless Sausages 101
Unknown Sprinters 104
References 107
The Big Teapot 110
Crubeens 114

Baking a Cake 118
Female Painters 123
Hair-oil 126
The Family History 129
Corner Boys 132
Potato-Cakes 135
Doors and Half-doors 139

THE GENTLE ART OF MATCHMAKING

A matchmaker is a man or woman practised in the gentle art of creating permanent alliances between men and women who might otherwise never participate in that long drawn-out confrontation known as marriage. For a short while I acted in such a capacity but it was only because the local matchmaker had passed on to his eternal reward as the place beyond the grave is hopefully called. I was neither a success nor a failure but I can proudly say that I was responsible for two marriages. One of the couples is blissfully happy but neither of the other have spoken to me since the knot was permanently tied. The male of the partnership in particular has it in for me and I have the fearful feeling that he is constantly endeavouring to whip up sufficient courage for one redoubtable, all-out assault.

Small blame to him for I am told that his spouse is incapable of silence for more than a second at a time. He has not spoken to her for several years and when he was chided by his father-in-law for this long lapse in communications he countered by saying that he didn't like interrupting her.

After this I gave up matchmaking and would refer aspiring martyrs to marriage bureaux or to experienced matchmakers who presided over other districts. To my mind a matchmaker is not unlike a judge whose painful duty it sometimes is to pass heavy sentences on those who appear before him. It is inevitable that those convicted by him will bear him ill-will and malice. It is the same with a matchmaker. It is he who caused the marriage in the first place. If the liason is happy all is well but if it is not he has passed a heavy sentence on two innocent people. They are not likely to forget him in a hurry. There are men I know who heartily detest the man or woman who first introduced them to the women who later became their wives. It is a thousand times worse in the case of a matchmaker and there are some I know who walk warily, always on the look-out for retaliation.

Personally I look upon marriage as a game, a very long game, of course. There are ups and downs, moments of great elation and deep depression, indiscretions, bouts of temper and what-have-you.

It is a game which requires only two contestants and there is no need for an umpire or a referee. Once the whistle is blown there can be no outside interference, no stopping of the play until one of the principals is called off the pitch by his or her maker. That is the final whistle for the partner in question but not for the one left on the field of play. One may start a new game with a new partner if one so desires and provided a new partner is available.

It is unquestionably the oldest game in the world and even those who have been punished and pummelled by its sometime rigours would not swop it for any other game. The tragedy is that there are millions of prospective players standing in the sidelines most anxious to participate but lacking the drive to dash into the game.

Here is where the gentle art of matchmaking comes into its own. Your astute fixer of lasting partnerships will look for teams that are evenly matched. Since there is only one player on each team this is not as difficult as it first may seem. The object in selecting teams which are evenly matched is to ensure that decisive victory never goes to either side, that there is draw after draw and replay after replay. Thus only can a game that is satisfying to both teams be assured.

Physical resemblance has little to do with it for I have often seen a seven-stone man outplay a fifteen-stone woman and I have seen a woman of five feet outfield a man of six feet three.

Where there is marriage tardiness in a village or townland there is an absolute necessity for a matchmaker. Where people are retiring and shy and incapable of speaking for themselves the matchmaker will do it for them. Maybe the result is not always heavenly bliss but a human voice is better than the four walls of an empty room, not to mention the cold of an empty bed.

Sometimes there are couples who have been courting for years but for one reason or another the vital question is never popped. Seasons pass and hair grows grey yet there is no suggestion that a marriage bed should be permantly shared. What is needed here is a prompt or a pinch or a push and the man best qualified to do this is your matchmaker.

I once heard of a couple who were walking out together for seven years but the male member of the firm never once hinted at marriage. Once when she said it would be nice to get married his reply was, 'who in God's name would marry the likes of us?' Not once did he give her a kiss or place an arm around her. One cold night they were sitting on a windy bridge when she complained of the cold.

'If my mother was here now', said the girl, 'she'd put an arm around me to save me from the cold'.

'Now, now', said the boyfriend, 'I can't be waking up your mother at this hour of the night'.

This is the way with many a couple. Time passes them

by. Their inability to take the plunge means that they must forego the thrills and spills of the greatest game known to man. That is why the art of matchmaking must never be allowed to die. It is a pauperised parish that cannot maintain or encourage one. We should all aspire to part-time matchmaking because the truth is that but for the matchmakers of yesterday many of us might not be here to-day.

A FAREWELL TO SALADS

Now that August has thrust it's tanned face into the picture of the year, I look forward eagerly to the days when there will be no more salads.

I have endured as many salad days as the next man and I have remained silent. However, I will not be pushed any further. Let there be a long respite from hard-boiled eggs and lettuce, from cucumber slices and adolescent onions for, after all, what is a salad but something you eat when it is too hot for anything else. It is not a meal. It is a replacement. It is a first sub who has been called in on too many occasions, a poor player with the best in togs and boots but oddly deficient in the finer points of football.

I had a granduncle who has long since emigrated to a more exhalted sphere. He was a small meticulous man who was always chronically short of cash. Despite this he maintained a good table and was a familiar figure in public-houses. The reason that I mention him is that he had a theory about lettuce and refused adamantly to countenance its presence in his house.

'Lettuce', he used to say, 'is sulky cabbage or, if you like, frustrated cabbage'.

He believed that if cabbages could talk they would have some very hard things to say about lettuce. I may have imbibed some of his prejudices because I too believe no self-respecting cabbage-head would be seen in the same garden as a bed of lettuce. This belief is founded on fact and if you do not go along with me just ask yourself what sort of company, outside the human species, you would like to be among in this planet. You would, of course, not opt for asses or corncrakes but for fellow humans however inconsequential or insufferable they may be. Cabbages, therefore, like to be seen among other cabbages.

'There's no veins in lettuce', my granduncle used to say. He would say this vehemently, daring whoever might be listening to disagree with him. Nobody ever did because everybody knew he was telling the truth. He did not have to convince me because even at that tender age I was an observant little fellow and without assistance from anybody was able to deduce that lettuce and its kindred components of the established salad were as big a bunch of chancers as ever I came across. Remember that I was a child of whom my mother used to say: 'He'll eat anything that's put in front of him'. This was not quite true but if you deduct the exaggeration to which mothers are addicted you may conclude that I was an individual who would eat almost anything. Fat meat, at which other children turned up their noses, was no problem to me. Corned beef, boiling beef, bacon, Irish stew . . . you name it and I've eaten it from an early age without a word of complaint. Rather it could be said that it was a pleasure to feed me. I was a harmonious little lad but even then, as now, I had a decided dislike for salads. Don't ask me why but the sight of them always made me feel disconsolate and if there are no good photographs of me as a child the salad must be blamed because summer time is photograph time and it's true to say that one is always either before or after a salad on a hot summer's day.

Why, then, are we in receipt of so many salads since it would appear that no briefs are held for them? How is it that, day after day, the salad takes his place on the table as if he were legitimately entitled to do so?

This is not going to be another of those unanswered questions. I could quite easily dodge the issue by changing the subject.

However, I believe that people should be informed. They should be enlightened, no matter who gets hurt in the process, so I will tell you without more ado that the heavy incidence of salads is due solely and exclusively to women.

Yes, women!

They do not like salads any more than you or I do but the arrangement and presentation of salads releases whatever artistry may be suppressed inside them. They love the colours of salads. The quality of the fare is secondary and they are delighted if they can deliver a plate which immediately catches the eye. My own beloved wife has on occasion presented me with a salad which boasted no fewer than nine different colours.

There were some glaring scarlet beetroots and late green peas which had been reserved from some long-forgotten dinner. There were slices of hardboiled eggs chalk-white with vivid orange centres. There were some dices of off-white potatoes and beryllene green cucumbers. The lettuce which dominated the colour scheme was a deeper green than the other greens, no doubt, one of the more strident in the forty shades in the song of that name.

But wait! I haven't finished. There were infinitisemal slices of pale pink carrots and finally there were several thin slices of vermilion red tomatoes. This is the reason why women look so long and so fondly at their plates of salad before they commence with the business of eating.

Take note that this little thesis is neither a salute nor a condemnation. I want it to be accepted as a farewell to salads.

THE CHINA HALF-SET

Many years ago, in a country kitchen, I sat with the woman of the house while she smoked a well-earned cigarette, having finished entertaining a troupe of demanding Yanks. In the middle of our conversation, a neighbour entered and planked himself down near the fire.

'I see', said he, 'that you're after having visitors'·

'How do you know that?' said the woman of the house who was irked at having to douse her cigarette prematurely.

'Because', said the newcomer, 'you have the room cups on the table'.

For the benefit of those who may not know what a room cup was, I should perhaps do a little explaining

They were part of the venerable, china half-set which rested, under lock and key, in the room cupboard. The room was a mixture of dining-hall, sittingroom and livingroom· Its facilities were never indulged in by the people of the house. It was reserved exclusively for visitors and Station breakfasts. The outstanding piece of furniture was a polished antique dresser, which was never opened. In it reposed the half-set of china I have mentioned. This half-set consisted of cups, saucers, side-plates, jug, and sugar-bowl, and, on isolated occasions, egg-cups. When the dresser was opened the protestations of its diminutive and underworked hinges were as loud and prolonged as the lamentations of a full-grown ban-

14

shee. Inside were many odds and ends ranging from last year's Christmas decorations to a special reserve of linen table-cloths.

The half-set of ware, however, was the first thing to catch the eye. There were houses where these half-sets were never used and they passed, unmolested and un-chipped, from generation to generation, growing in value and prestige. They became so hallowed in the end that it would be sacrilegious to expose them on a kitchen table. The half-sets were the pride and joy of the women who owned them and if a caller were important enough they were extracted with great care to honour his visisations. 'Love me; love my china!' was the motto of the woman who preserved them and it was more important to praise the cup than its contents. A cute man might say: 'By Gor, that's as nice a set of ware as ever I saw!' or, 'Aren't you foolish to be using these missus? I'm sure they're worth a small fortune!' A man who made re-marks like these was sure to be defended thereafter should his name be drawn down derogatorily in the course of conversation. Younger men who praised half-sets were regarded as desirable sons-in-law.

With all due respects to insurance agents, postmen, and Guards, they never qualified for tea out of these delicate cups. They were almost exclusively exposed to the discerning appraisal of Yanks, parish priests and maternity nurses.

As time went by, bits and pieces were added to the half-sets so that if a well-loved guest admired a particular item he, or she, was made a present of it before leav-ing the house. But this custom has died out. It was common. I am told, in Afghanistan and Venezuela for a visitor to be presented with a piece of home-made pott-ery which took his fancy during a meal, which goes to show that basically people are the same the world over.

15

Once, after a meal which consisted of two boiled eggs, I admired the design on the egg-cup and was presented with it, wrapped in butter-paper, as I was about to depart.

Another country woman of my aquaintance, who owned a pedigree set of china ware, had, at a jumble sale in the town, invested in two small china mugs which she dearly cherished. On each was written: 'Think of me when this you see'. She gave them both away without a moment's hesitation to my own spouse, who chanced to admire them when she was on a visit and it is true to say that whenever we look at them we think of her.

When the half-set saw long periods of idleness it was taken from its sanctuary and washed carefully with soap and water. The woman of the house would permit nobody to participate in this operation. 'If one is broken', she would say, 'I have no one but myself to blame' and it was rare indeed that a piece of the set was chipped or broken. The best thing to do if a saucer cracked or a cup fractured itself was to vacate the house immediately and take refuge with a neighbour until she cooled off.

Many wise housewives had two half-sets. There was the commoner, which was used for visitors, and the reserve, which was never used at all unless a bishop happened to call. This latter set was for show and while it was permissible to admire it, you daren't take a piece in your hands.

Housewives of all shapes and sizes, regardless of their years, will never pass a window where sets of china are exhibited. Regardless of their hurry they must pause to cast a longing look inwards. They will pass windows of frocks, shoes and hats when hurry urges them but a temptingly arranged set of ware is too much for them·

It all began, I daresay, when they were presented with

16

their first set of doll's ware. After that it was only a matter of time before they set their eyes on the man they wanted and the china half-set to match him.

COMPOSITIONS

These pieces in this book may be loosly described as compositions. Nowadays I get paid for writing them but time was when I was forced to do them for nothing for my English teachers. I didn't mind. They were patient, easy-going men who got the best out of a fellow in the long run. I wasn't very good in those days, being hampered by a vivid imagination and a chronic shortage of knowledge, grammar, and vocabulary. But, be that as it may, there were others in my class who were as bad as I was. There were good fellows, too, who did everything correctly and made no mistake but, good as they were, their compositions were bloodless, lifeless, and gutless. It was always the bad fellow who made the headlines.

There was, when I was in the National School, a boy of eleven who was easily the greatest writer of compositions I ever met. If I say he inspired me I do him an injustice. Rather I should say he enchanted me. He coloured my days and all our days including the teacher's.

This boy did not believe in sentences. Commas and full-stops he belittled and he loathed semi-colons.

'What do I want with them', he said to me one evening after school, 'when they only gets in my way'.

When he started a composition he never finished. He went on until he was stopped and I know that he would have gone on writing for ever if they had let him. His composition was like the ride of Young Lochinar with minor amendments.

> He stayed not for syntax nor grammar nor pun
> And save his good pencil he weapons had none·

Page after page was filled and he never once looked about him as he wrote with furious abandon. It was as if he was determined to use up all the writing paper in the world. Yet, long as his composition was, it was all made up of one mighty sentence. When the teacher would examine it afterwards and say: 'I can't make head nor tail of this', the composer would blush modestly and hang his head with true humility. I once read one of his better efforts. He scorned the subject and wandered off in all directions with strange descriptions of football matches, cowboy pictures and street fights. Only one word in five was spelled correctly· There were no full stop, no comma. Nothing interfered with his fantastic flow. The overall composition was always highly entertaining although one would need a skeleton key if one did not know him personally.

He was only one of many. There was another who scorned spelling and when he ran out of big words he invented his own. One of his best creations was a word called 'dihiderophantic'.

'You won't find this word in any dictionary', the teacher announced when he read the composition.

'They must have forgot to put it in', the composer suggested·

'That must be it', said the teacher, 'but maybe you'll be good enough to tell us what it means'.

'It don't mean nothing', said the composer.

When we went to secondary school the subjects of the compositions became more abstract and we were faced with doing seven hundred words on 'Thrift',' Happiness', and others of a like.

One brilliant young mind who is now more than likely saying Mass in some part of South America was more daring than any of us. The subject was 'Thrift' and the teacher had told us that we should not be afraid to write what we felt. Our friend was selected for special mention when all the essays were finished.

His last sentence dealt with assiduous savers: 'every one of them is lousers,' he wrote.

When we got to the Leaving certificate stage we got swanky and started to call our compositions 'essays'.

We were a bit more sensible and a bit more careful and there was no more fun. No, there was nothing to whack the National School composition for sheer bravado and originality. I wish I had a hundred of them before me to pass away the night.

GAMBLES

The gamble is a thing of the past.

Too much money for one thing and too many motors
for another.

I once participated in a gamble for a fat goose. There
were eight of us at the table and knaves were cast to see
who would partner whom. The game was '31' or, if you
like, '25', with 11 for the best trump. Our group qualified
for the final and there was an air of tension in the kitchen
as the cards were shuffled. The issue was to be decided
on the best of five games. In short, the first man to win
three games would be the outright winner of the goose.

Cards were cut for the deal and I drew lowest. The
man next to me was warned to watch his cut in case
I had 'put them together'. As the games progressed
there were sighs and groans. Knaves were ruthlessly
struck by fives and aces of hearts fell foul of knaves.
Diamonds were kept but to no avail. Luck was the de-
ciding element and finally the game was won by a man
with a cap on his head and a week's beard on his face.
He won it on the last day's trick and he hit the table
a resounding belt of his fist as he did so. It would have
been sacrilegious to win the trick silently.

Post-mortems were held, but it was agreed that he had
played his cards well. 'Kind for him', said one old woman, 'all belongin' to him was gamblers'. It transpired
that he had won a turkey the year before at a '25' drive
in Templeglantine and went to the last four in Athea

when a tractor of dry turf was at stake.

There are still gambles for turkeys, geese and hams, but the days of the big gambles are gone. I do not mean that the prize was enormous when I say big gambles. I mean that a widow-woman's gamble was as important a social event as the Stations. Contestants paid a shilling a head and when the prize was won there was tea and bread and jam. Afterwards there was a bit of a dance. There were rows, too, occasionally but these were accepted as the natural hazards of the course. Suspected renegers were challenged with all the passion of the Old West and if there weren't six-shooters there were bony knuckles eager to tip a tune on the defaulter's head.

Some were not above concealing the ace of hearts, most versatile of cards in a waistcoat pocket or trousers-fold and it was all right as long as you got away with it. In fact, those who suceeded in breaking the rules successfully were regarded as dare-devils and were looked upon as lovable characters as long as they weren't caught out.

Keeping the game in was an art in itself and woe to him who didn't stick the high man. The fall of the lift was always in but today it is no longer observed. I daresay there are enough restrictions in the world without adding to them.

When the cards were put away the kettle went down and cups appeared. There were no saucers since it was only to be 'a cup out of the hand'. There were several loaves of shop bread specially bought for the occasion and there were two or three large pots of mixed fruit jam. Jam was regarded as a treat in those days because I remember a farmer's boy who once complained about his diet to his mistress. 'Maybe', she said sarcastically, ' 'tis bread and jam you expect?'

Gambles generally began a week before Christmas

and there was never a night without one. A man would get word that he was expected to play for a goat in Knockanure on Thursday night and he was warned by messengers not to miss the turkey in Carrickerry on Friday night. I once knew a man who cycled twenty-seven miles to play for a goat. He told me so himself. Goats were valuable acquisitions. The skin was used to make a bodhran for the Wren-boys on Saint Stephen's Day and the meat was given to greyhounds. It was supposed to be good for no-course duffers and three-quarters. A three-quarters was a dog who looked like a greyhound and ate like a greyhound but who failed to perform like a greyhound.

There were gambles for greyhound pups and holy pictures, gambles for she-goats and pucks, asses and ponies, cows and calves, turkeys, geese and bonhams. These last were mostly pet bonhams and difficult to rear unless there was an old woman in the house who understood their ways. 'Twas often that the ioctar of the litter turned out, in the end, to be the best of all.

There were times when local blackguards would come along while the gamble was in progress and stuff the chimney of the house with a wet sack. The kitchen was quickly filled with smoke and it was always wise to count the cards after incidents like these.

The gamble is gone, all right, but it's heyday will come again when people realise that the best joys are simple joys.

THE PAPERS

I like newspapers!

I like their shape, rustle and content and whether the headlines concern themselves with twin-calves or the utterance of forged cheques it is of no matter to me because every page is virgin territory and there is always the possibility that in some obscure corner there is good news about oneself or one's friends.

There is bad news too but some newspapers have souls and they knock most of the harm out of it. For instance I remember, some years ago, there was a court case involving a woman who took sausages from a shop-counter without paying for them. That she was a chronic offender in this respect never came to light. She was fined ten shillings and bound over. The following evening the story appeared in the newspapers. One was particularly kind. A small headline ran: 'Sick woman suffers from lapse of memory'.

Another time a man was convicted of stealing an ass-rail of turf from a farmer who had a rick in the depths of the bog. He was caught in the act after the farmer had complained of previous thefts to the Civic Guards. In court he was fined thirty shillings and told that he would be jailed for any further offence. The justice commented, as justices are wont to do, that this was a particularly mean type of offence. The excuse put forward by the defendant was that he mistook the farmer's rick for his own and that he trusted to the instincts of his donkey to guide him to the right rick. A weekly paper carried the story a few days later. The facts were there but the headline was a gem: 'Turfman duped by donkey'.

Whenever an unlikely type comes to me looking for the loan of a paper which is not sold locally, I am immediately on my guard. In the first place the caller does not strike me as a reader of newspapers and the first question I ask is: 'Why do you want it?' Invariably the answer is: 'Oh, there's something about so-and-so in it'. If it was something good there would be no demand for the paper so I have to conclude that it is something bad.

People are strange and just when you think you've gotten to know them they become stranger still. The majority gloat, with charitable sighs, on the misfortunes of others.

In the town where I live it could be said that I am relatively popular which is about as popular as anybody can hope to be. Anyway, if you become too popular you build up a dangerous opposition whose aim is to bring you down. Some years ago a play of mine was performed in Dublin and I bought the four morning papers to read the reviews. Three of the reviews were quite good and one was bad, very bad, so bad in fact that it was almost defamatory

Around about that time the papers came out a stranger called to see me. He congratulated me on the reviews and said my friends and fellow townspeople would be pleased. I told him that he was probably right, but not altogether, and I explained to him that the paper which had the bad review would be sold out in a matter of minutes. He refused to believe me and we had a substantial bet. We waited an hour and, sure enough, when we went out to the several newsagents to purchase a copy of the paper there wasn't one to be had. I wasn't in the least bit disappointed because if you know people you know they can be like that.

It is a foolish man who, having committed some misdemeanor, approaches the paper not to publish the story about him. No self-respecting newspaper will pay any attention to him but there are times when, because of mighty pressure, it can be done. This is a mistake and almost worse than front-page headlines because the story is left to the imagination and people will confide to one another that it must have been a terrible deed altogether if it was so bad that it couldn't appear in the newspapers.

Other people, mostly women, borrow newspapers for other purposes, if not to wrap eggs or odd cups then to clip slip or cardigan patterns from their pages. There is no mention of why the newspaper is wanted when it is being borrowed but when it is returned there are large scissors-made gaps which often drive the owner to distraction.

A man with a newspaper in his pocket is as formidable as a man with a pipe in his mouth. It doesn't matter whether he is capable of reading the newspaper or not. What matters is that he can carry it so that part of it juts out of the pocket with the discretion of a shirtcuff.

Most people rarely bother with the front page of newspapers. They investigate the innards where the real meat is. Anyhow, front pages are nearly always taken up with nuclear explosions or aeroplane crashes and when you know about one nuclear explosion you know about them all.

When I get my paper I like it fresh and unruffled. I hate if anybody else reads it before me as this knocks half the value out of it. It really doesn't matter, I know, but there is a psychological explanation somewhere, not to be found in the pages of newspapers.

Reading a newspaper on board a train is a bit like

watching a film in a strange cinema. The same amount of satisfaction is never derived from it. One must be in familiar surroundings and it is safer to challenge a bull-elephant than it is to interrupt a man who is interested in his newspaper.

TROTTERS

The unusual holds a fascination for everybody but if only we were prepared to reflect we would discover that what we believe to be unusual is quite commonplace and, in fact, deserves no mention at all. Take for example those numerous parents who see in their own children the embodiment of all that is unique, beautiful, and talented and who see nothing at all in the child next door who may have ten times the talent and ability. Old carpers who are fond of knocking these treatises of mine will ask 'what's he at now?'

Patience, dear readers, and you shall see. It must be plain to all that I will shortly be writing about some thing or body which is unusual, which, in short, is well worthy of the comments I propose to make.

I was present some months ago at a football game. I was one of many hundreds who had come to pass away an hour or so watching a sport dear to us all. The teams took the field after the usual delay and after a brief inspection plus a short lecture by the referee the whistle was blown and the game was on. It started at a cracking pace and there were several minutes of unbroken play which had the crowd on their toes and the majority cheering wildly for one side or the other. It is at moments like these when all eyes are fixed on the commonplace that mine are drawn away to look for the unusual. It is a good time for people are somewhat uninhibited and behavior is truly normal.

There was nothing exceptional about the crowd or about the wheeling seagulls overhead. The elements themselves were as normal as they might be for the time of year. My eyes were about to return to the field of play when they were arrested by a movement at the other side of the field. It was the linesman dashing to and fro. He was never still and was the antithesis of our own linesmen who never left the same position lest his enjoyment of the game be interrupted. He was one of those experienced and cunning officials who sees the ball go over the line but does absolutely nothing except wait to see how the majority of the players behave. If the majority move downfield he will indicate with his flag that the free is to be downfield and vice versa if the majority move upfield. If there is the slightest contention he will throw in the ball himself. Before we begin to despise this type of linesman let us remember that he is in favour of majority rule although some of the majority may come from sideline support. But to press on; the linesman at the opposite side was a tireless fellow and extremely conscientious to boot. He was the epitome of vigilance, a quantity, incidentally, for which sideline men receive more abuse than thanks.

Looking at him stirred my memory and it occurred to me that his behaviour was different from all other linesmen I had seen over the years. I could not quite make out what it was that made him different but different he was and there could be no doubt about that. I watched him more closely and, ever anxious to improve the mind and add to the store of knowledge, I waited till half-time when he came across to our side.

It was only then that it dawned on me what he was. It took time but there could be no mistaking that lifting of the leg, that kick of the feet when he made haste and finally, conclusively that way he held his head in the air.

This man was a trotter. In stature he was small as almost all trotters are. In addition, his legs were short and if devastating proof were needed, which it isn't, his posterior was very near the ground.

In short, he had all the classic points of the true trotter. Incidentally, trotters are very rare. The world is full of gallopers and trudgers but the trotter is so rare that one could spend an entire lifetime without meeting one.

After the match he trotted towards the exit. Notice I say trotted and not walked. Many there were who walked and some there were who ran but only he of all who were there was prepared to trot.

When I say he trotted I do not wish to imply that he was in a hurry or that he moved faster than most. He moved at a pace which was just a trifle faster than a good walk. All the time the head was held high and all the time his pace was even. Outside the ground he trotted towards his car and as he opened the door I could almost swear I heard a whinny in the far distance beyond our yesterdays.

I haven't seen a trotter since but I am always on the look-out for one. Be on the look-out for a man with the points I have noted and one day you, too, may see a real, live trotter.

SOCKS

Only a dunderhead will ask his wife for a fresh pair of socks on a Sunday morning.

The wise man who knows his womenfolk will settle his affairs the night before and wake in an independent frame of mind on the morning of the Sabbath.

Women, for some secret reason of their own, never seem to take on single pairs of socks. When they darn they darn every damned thing they can find. Nothing is sacred, not even the most ancient and shrunken of hose, long retired from the unequal struggle against vigorous heels and toes.

There is no point in telling a woman that a certain pair of socks have grown too small. A woman with a darning needle in her hand has a mission in life. Her aim is to pile up a great dump of socks against the rainy day and she is not concerned about shape or size.

She means well but socks like husbands, need constant attention.

Luckily for mankind there is a type of shop which may be knocked up with impunity on Sundays. Here bundles of socks lie between cards of one-and-sixpenny penknives and pounds of loose rice. They may be buried underneath mounds of mixed herbs and senna leaves but the important thing is that they are there and a little patience will see them unearthed.

There may be a good reason why women darn socks whose vamps have grown too small. Whatever it is I refuse to listen to it. I have seen backyards littered with rejected pairs that have been thrown out of rear windows by exasperated husbands who have issued warnings for the last time. Do not be hasty to condemn the man who is reluctant about making room in his pew on Sunday for, without doubt, the vamps of his socks are too small for him and his humour is a long way from being restored.

Perhaps the most unfair demand ever made upon the average husband is to send him rooting for socks on his own when he needs a pair most.

'Where are they?' he'll shout.

'They're there in the bag in the press', he will be told. He will search diligently without success.

"Try the drawer!' he will be told.

'Which drawer?' he will call in exasperation.

'The drawer where they always are!' the answer will come back.

I have seen the kindest of men break up after ten minutes of such treatment. I have watched staid, sober fathers being transformed into fiends at the monstrous futility of their endeavours. But the point of no return is reached when she fails to locate them herself and says: 'Why don't you tell me in advance when you want socks and not be always leaving things go till the last minute?'

The happiest of marriages have been threatenea, not by overboiled potatoes or gritty gravy, but by lost unattached collars and missing socks but, whereas an unattached collar can be turned inside out, there is no such alternative with the gutted sock. If a sock has a hole on the outside then by all powers that be it also has a hole on the inside. Odd socks with contrasting colours are better than holed socks or shrunken socks and I will lay odds that all the house-wives who are listening to this are aware of the following irrefutable facts:

1. There are socks in your house at this moment which have shrunken far beyond the measure of your man's foot and yet you persist in holding on to them;
2. There are widowed socks in your house whose partners are gone beyond recall and yet you keep them, thereby encouraging a serious marital rift at a later date;
3. There are socks in your house with more darns than original material, yet you hang on;
4. There are socks in your house with such colour schemes of mixed darning that the eye is dazzled by the sight of them but will you throw them out? You will not.

But enough, I could go on forever.

The secret about socks is that they should be bought as often as possible. The woman who buys two pairs of socks today and none for weeks is at fault but the woman who buys one pair today and another pair at every opportunity has a fighting chance of keeping up with the demand. She is at least making an effort.

I know of a woman who once darned white socks with black thread and, when her husband protested, she said, 'My goodness, aren't we getting very particular?'

An army may march on its stomach but it is the sock that carries the foot and it is the foot which carries the stomach. A man cannot have enough socks in his home and by socks I mean socks that will fit and not socks that infuriate. In the race of life man is often told that he will have to pull up his socks or be left behind but how can a man pull up his socks if they refuse to stretch beyond his ankles?

SPECTACLES

It was at a district football meeting, many years ago, that I had my first harrowing encounter with a pair of horn-rimmed spectacles·

Our club was objecting to a referee who, we felt, would damage our prospects in a forthcoming final. Had we not objected then the opposing team would have done so but now that we were first in the field they opposed us just for pure spite.

I was elected spokesman for our club, not because I was wiser than my fellows, but because I was younger and nobody else wanted the job. I pointed out that the referee in question was not above taking large quantities of strong drink before matches and this frequently interfered with his judgment.

The chairman, who wore a pair of black horn-rimmed glasses looked at me sagely and I was tricked into going on.

'I have seen him', I said, 'award a penalty when the foul was committed in the middle of the field and when the mistake was pointed out to him, he sent the man who told him to the sideline'.

Then the spokesman for the other team rose and insisted that these were very serious charges and that the referee in question, while he might have a small alcoholic weakness, was nevertheless reliable and well informed on the finer points of the game.

When my opponent sat down the chairman took off

his spectacles and put one of the rims into his mouth. He chewed the rim for a while and seemed to enjoy the flavour. When the course was finished he withdrew the first rim and put the other into his mouth. Instead of chewing this rim he sucked it as a child might a lollipop.

He sucked it for a considerable time but on this occasion displayed no particular love for the taste. He withdrew the rim and then skilfully twirled the spectacles in his right hand. He transferred them to his left hand and scratched behind his right ear with one of the rims.

It was an impressive performance. He was showing that justice was not to be done lightly; that he was bringing all the powers of his intellect to bear upon the problem.

Suddenly, holding the glasses by one rim, he pointed the spectacles in my direction: 'My dear man', said he, 'you don't know what you're talking about'.

Then, without further ado, he found in favour of the opposition, after which he explained, at great length, that he liked a drink himself and asked, with a flourish of the spectacles, if the country was reduced to such a state that it condemned innocent men for taking a drink.

I quickly interrupted and said my club had no objection to his drinking after the match but we strongly objected to his drinking before the match.

At this the chairman put on his glasses to get a better look at me. Quickly, however, he took them off again, leaning back in his chair made a wide arc with the glasses and ended by holding a rim in each hand as if he were going to put them on.

But he didn't put them on. He looked through them from a distance as if there were a letter of instructions written on the lenses.

'My dear man', he said, without raising his head, 'in this country a man can drink whatever he likes, wherever he likes and whenever he likes!'

This was greeted by a loud burst and handclapping. In fact I noticed some of my own team-mates clapping.

It suddenly dawned on me that I hadn't a hope against this man while he could use his spectacles to embellish his announcements. There was nothing I could do but withdraw my objection.

But it taught me a lesson.

I resolved that, as soon as possible, I would have a pair of spectacles of my own, horn-rimmed ones if possible. Time passed and one day an eye specialist found me guilty of blurred vision.

He sentenced me to a pair of new spectacles and since the first time I donned them I have never lost an argument. I let the spectacles do the work. When a difficult question is popped, I take them off, produce my handkerchief and commence polishing the lenses. This takes so long that somebody else always answers the question before I am finished.

Beware, dear readers, of a man who sucks the ends of the rims. He is a dangerous adversary and will stop at nothing to achieve his aims. He will go as far as to bite rims and, if you examine his spectacles, you will notice the notches made by his teeth.

These notches are victory notches. Instead of grinning hugely, which is the orthodox thing to do, he will conceal his emotions by biting his spectacles.

But he has more shots in his sling than that. It is when he takes off his glasses and inspects them closely, as if he were searching for flaws, that he is at his most dangerous. He does this only when he is cornered and a cornered spectacle-wearer has much the same instincts as a cornered water-buffalo.

The only advice I can proffer about entering a debate with this type of man is to steal his glasses before the contest begins.

PERIWINKLES

Is there nourishment in periwinkles?

The question was put to me recently by a young man with an inquiring mind. It is a question which a scholar might dismiss and one which might offend the professional dietician but young men who thirst for knowledge should not be discouraged.

The periwinkle is a gastropod or whelk found in great abundance on rocky coasts between tides. Periwinkle-picking is a way of life largely dependent on the soles and toes of the feet and to a lesser degree on the eyesight.

The periwinkle himself is an inoffensive chap, not given to conversation. He is not excitable as are crabs and lobsters and he is not aggressive. There is no known instance of assault by periwinkle. He clings patiently to a black rock waiting for the picker to come along. He is then boiled with thousands of his fellows and allowed to cool. Even in death he retains the small circular hat which is the traditional headgear of his family.

He is eaten with the teeth but he is abducted from his shell with the common pin and those who are fond of such fare generally over-indulge themselves. Hence the great demand at seaside resorts, cattle-fairs and horseraces. Most youngsters take to periwinkles as a duck takes to water and many prefer them to fish-and-chips, crisps and ice-cream.

But back to the original question.

Is there nourishment in the periwinkle? I am inclined to think that the answer is . . . yes! The bother now is to prove it.

First let me say that the periwinkle is a more rugged customer than his cousin, the landlubber snail so beloved of the French and Belgians. The French have won some renown in the matter of food-tasting and the snail is the national dish of that country. He is held in high esteem and is thought to be sufficient in himself as a provider of sustenance and energy. If the periwinkle then is a better specimen than this much-lauded Frenchie – and I think we have agreed that he is – it must be admitted that he occupies a very high place in the international food register.

Vitamin is a work which keeps cropping up unexpectedly when unusual foods are under discussion. How docs the periwinkle stand in respect of the vitamin? Does he know his A.B.C. and does he compare favourably with prescribed foods which are recommended by authoritative sources. He does possess vitamins A.B.C. and he also possesses another extremely rare vitamin which has not yet made the charts but which is likely candidate for the Top Ten in any country·

For want of a better name I shall call this vitamin The Gimp. Most people know what a gimp is but for the benefit of those who do not I had better explain. A gimp is what a man gets after three or four pints of stout. It may be a gimp for fighting and it may be a gimp for a meal. Sometimes it may be a gimp for women. This does not mean that every adult male who eats perwinkles publicly is carrying a half-gallon cargo of stout. It merely suggests it because many adults will have the periwinkle with or without stout.

The gimp, therefore, is a vitamin of consequence and

I think it can be concluded that there are several gimps in the average periwinkle.

The periwinkle possesses another vitamin which all other shellfish lack and this is to be found in his tail which is the tenderest part of him and a part which is often, unfortunately, lost in the shell by inexperienced pickers. I am at a loss as to how this vitamin should be described. The tail of the periwinkle tastes differently from the top or trunk and is rich in proteins but it is the particular vitamin which is peculiar to the tail that matters. If I may do so, I would like to call it Vitamin P.2. You may ask 'Why P.2.?' Well, the P. stands for periwinkle and the 2 stands for the tail. If there is a more appropriate name I should like very much to know what it is but I will be greatly surprised if there is.

I have eaten as many periwinkles as anybody. Man and boy, I must have accounted for a cool hundred thousands of these delectable tit-bits although tit-bits is hardly a fitting title.

Notice how I have made no attempt in this treatise to defend the periwinkle. Dumb though he may be, he speaks eloquently for himself. From his beretted noodle to his little curly tail he is tasty and delicious.

A time may come when he will be preserved and put in tins or glass jars but I doubt if he will taste the same. He is at his best in his shell. After all it is his home and a man is always at his best on his own doorstep. Take him out of his environment and he is never the same. Personally speaking, I will never lose the tooth for periwinkles· I was reared on them and I will not readily forget the first time that I could afford to buy a whole bag out of my own pocket. I felt a sense of achievement and importance because there is an air of independence about a man who eats his periwinkles in public.

40

THE ASS AND CART

The other day I was intrigued by a notice which appeared in a provincial newspaper: 'Wanted: a donkey's cart, complete with seat and guards, condition immaterial'.

I put it down to the work of a hopeful sentimentalist for he might have more profitably advertised for 'A young man to handle lions and tigers; no experience necessary'. I am left wondering if he received an answer but, frankly, I doubt if he did. There are still plenty of donkey carts but the 'sate and guard' is a thing of the past. Those of us whose grandmothers sat airily on those throne-like seats will never forget the dignity of a shawled old lady and the status she could give to this most humble and most ancient of conveyances· Invariably the donkey was a rougue but his every idiosncrasy was known to his aged charioteer who possessed an insight into the antics of pampered asses which was nothing short of a revelation.

The ass and car is still used to carry milk to the creamery and the ass and rail is without peer when the turf is stranded in squelchy bogs but, as a means of transport, the woman of today will have nothing to do with it. Only the old-age pensioner will sit astride the rickety perch or plonk herself bravely between the shaft and the body of the car. She and her conveyance are more sought after than celebrities by camera-laden tourists and in many a Boston drawing room she hangs, aloof and serene, between outsize prints of Pope John and John Kennedy. She is not camera-shy and neither is her donkey, and if a dollar bill comes her way now and then, it is only her due. After all, isn't she a relic of the old days when emigration was a respectable profession and homecoming a highlight of the parochial year?

The donkey and cart offers a livelihood of another kind in the butterfly days of summer. A clever mother will dress her young in patched trousers and scrub their faces till they are spotless, put them into an ass cart and send them up and down a road which leads to a tourist resort. No better tourist bait exists unless we are to credit the presence of leprechauns· A crabit youngster with an appropriate expression of angelic innocence will earn more than his father in the round of a day and if he is experienced he will not be forgotten by departed holiday-makers when Christmas comes around. A good combination of cart, donkey and youngster is as big an attraction as a round tower or a Celtic cross, and I have often seen as many as three carloads of tourists at a time surrounding a single cart with cameras clicking like mowing-machines. An interested onlooker will hear expressions like: 'Well did you ever see anything so quaint!' or 'Gee, he's a real cute burro!' I know of many cases where the ass is retired when the season is over and the cart is carefully oiled and kept in cold storage until the grass grows long and the bone-dry dust is on the roads of Summer.

Sometimes when I sit in a speeding motor-car, I secretly long for an ass and cart. I do not mention this to the driver because he might well slow down and tell me that he has no objection and wholeheartedly approves of the change. I am cheered by the unhurried progress and the safe consistency of plopping hooves.

I am cheered as Xenophon's mercenaries were cheered when they encountered the hoofmarks of asses on their way back from the Persian campaign. These asses were wild asses but the hoofmarks, no doubt, brought back memories to those weary men; memories of shawled mothers in carts on their way to the cross roads in some mountainy corner of Greece. I can see Xenophon, now exhausted. He sits on a stone and wishes he were at home tackling the ass to take his grandfather to the Olympics.

Should you see three ass and carts together in this day and age it does not mean that a chariot race is about to begin. It means that the day is Friday and that the weekly trek for the old-age pension is under way.

There is no safer means of travel and I have lost count of the number of times I met a drowsy old man or woman who had a half-whiskey too many. The reins hung loosely over the donkey's neck but the ass clung religiously to his appointed portion of the roadway, surely a classic example of teamwork· In the cart his charge slept soundly and the only instructions passed on to the donkey were the occasional indecipherable snores. Home was always reached safely and will you tell me who remembers a fatal accident involving a a donkey and cart. If there are such accidents they are never the fault of the donkey. More than likely they are the fault of the two-legged donkey in charge of the motor-car. The two-legged donkey is an astonishing animal. Put him behind the wheel of a car and his powers of reasoning desert him. He lacks the patience of his four-footed brother who always gets where he wants to go without mishap or disaster·

Should there be a fine week this summer I would recommend a leisurely trip through the little-known roads of the country in a donkey and cart. The donkey is not a choosy feeder and will fend for himself among the roadside grasses. Don't carry a stick or a whip. Give him his head and in his own good time he will go places. A quarter stone of oats, now and then, will rise a gallop without urging. An ass's gallop is as smooth as airplane travel and as unpredictable. The difference is that when the donkey stops unexpectedly, you will be still seated in the cart.

Inevitably a tourist in an ass and car will be regarded as a curiosity and many well-meaning souls will mistake it for a publicity stunt. Rest assured that the ass will not be ruffled by comment or curiosity. His job is to pull the cart as his father and mother before him did and his indifferent assurance can be heart-warming when a horn hoots outrageously as if it were sole proprietor of the public road.

RIBBONS

Around her neck she wore a yellow ribbon
She wore it for her sweetheart in the U.S. Cavalry.
— (SONG)

On the way out of Mass last Sunday I was amazed to discover that not a single ribbon was worn by any member of the gentle sex.

Times have certainly changed when we remember the anguish of the young lady who waited so long for Johnny's return from the fair.

Johnny had promised to bring back a bunch of blue ribbons to tie up her bonny brown hair. The young lady was heard to say: 'Oh, dear, what can the matter be?' while she waited with her pretty face pressed against the window pane for the return of her sweetheart.

When I first heard that song years ago I was deeply worried also and I feared for Johnny's safe return, what with highwaymen and the high incidence of accidents from potholes. Now, of course, I realise that Johnny was never in danger and I can see the picture clearly. The Johnny of those days was no different from the Johnny of these days who goes to a coursing meeting or a football match. It is now obvious that he met a few of the boys and completely forgot about the ribbons·

It is the gullibility and innocence of Johnny's young sweetheart which intrigues me. Many of our modern young ladies would not have been content to wait so patiently and it is doubtful if a brown paper bag full of ribbons would be sufficient to mollify them if one fell among evil companions. By evil companions I mean those characters who are the life and soul of public-house singsongs.

I will concede that I do come across rosy-cheeked damsels of six and seven whose hair is almost always bedecked with gay ribbons, but what about our older misses — the rockers, the hoppers, and the twisters? What have they got against ribbons? Perry Como sings a song about scarlet ribbons and I have it on good authority that Elvis Presley likes a good ribbon. In spite of this, however, ribbons are regarded as being quaint and old-fashioned. Most ballet-dancers wear ribbons when they practice in their skintight outfits and it is worth noting that most ballet-dancers succeed in ending up with wealthy husbands.

In my opinion all the hats in the world are not to be compared to a bright silk ribbon tightly bound about the brow. The effect is neat and endearing and there is that Hiawatha-like look which hairdressers have tried to copy, without success, for generations.

A little while ago I mentioned that I was writing about ribbons to an old lady of my acquaintance. She told me that she had a large box of multicoloured ribbons when she was a young girl and for special occasions a smaller box of striped ribbons. There was a practice, too, of swopping ribbons, much the same way as youngsters swop comics and there was a good deal of jealousy caused by unusual ribbons much the same as hairstyles and hats these days. Confirmations and Communions were the annual showtimes of the ribbon and special parcels of ribbon were sent home by rela-tives in America. Shop windows were alight with huge rolls of slim, delightfully-coloured ribbons and when a suit of clothes or an overcoat or a frock were purchased it was an impoverished draper who didn't throw in a yard or two of ribbon for good measure. There were odd ribbons or spare ribbons in colourful little bunches which could be bought for as little as tuppence at all high-class emporiums.

But do our young ladies gather ribbons in this day and age? No, sir! They prefer the growing pile of pop-records which do not contain a single song about ribbons but it is fair to say that ribbons will be there when all the pop-records are forgotten.

There is nothing as bright and colourfully contagious as the bow-knot of a good ribbon and nothing so nostalgic as a song about ribbons. They symbolised purity and chastity and evil could not triumph where they reigned. They were truly girlish and they were without pretension. Most important, they were within the scope for all. For a few pence a drab head could be transformed into a garden of coloured confusion. Hearts were uplifted and the spirits rose at the sight of them. They were the next best thing to rays of sunshine and the rain looked lighter around the heads on which they flourished.

There is something about a girl who wears a ribbon, hard to put a finger on, a sort of defiant gaiety, a kind of refusal to be intimidated by misfortune, a kind of gay courage which must prevail when times are bad and pockets are empty. It is next to impossible to define it but I think it could be admitted that a girl who wears a ribbon is a real girl. Yes, that's it — a real girl.

Anything that makes the world a little brighter is worth encouraging and, as a man said to me lately, 'they're cheaper than hats'.

BOHAREENS

Oh, I do like to wander down the old bohareen
When the hawthorn blossoms are in bloom ...
— (SONG)

One of the great tragedies of this modern age is that people do not go walking down bohareens any more.

They don't walk up bohareens either, because one must go down to come up.

The dictionary has words for those who explore caves and collect coins, but there is no word for the bohareen-walker. All around us are little roads and grass-covered, rutted tracks that lead to nowhere. There should be a society for the preservations of bohareens or, if this is not possible, each of us who have an interest in what is simple and good in life should adopt a bohareen. Nothing could be less expensive for all that has to be done is to repulse take-over bids from companies like Briars and Nettles and Thistles and Docks and to encourage small businesses like the Wild Rose and the Buttercup.

Walking down bohareens is a must for those who find members of the opposite sex endearing and a man who hasn't walked down a bohareen with his best girl has missed much. Those couples who haven't held hands and skipped a bit between high whitethorn hedges had better do so at once, not for my sake but for their own. Who knows what woes will taint the winds of coming

48

summers and, after all, we're only young once. Now in the time and who knows better than those of us who dallied with sweethearts of yesterday that we are travelling on a one-way ticket in this topsy-turvy world and truly the man who has paid his dues to bohareens can say when his hair, if any is grey: for me the past has no regrets for I am one who has honoured the little roads that lead to nowhere.

I myself have not given up bohareen-walking and I know a few good ones where children can be nurtured to appreciation, where the only traffic is the annual hay-car and the only life the occasional donkey without portfolio. The bohareen is the last sanctuary of overworked ponies absent without leave, rogue nanny-goats, hare-shy greyhounds, indisposed hedgehogs, and other unseen creatures who prefer the cloistered quiet of grassy ways to the tumult of terror-laden thoroughfares.

The bohareen is a refuge, a haven for harried souls who like to amble along safe from the noisome jarring of carhorns and the sudden death that their absence precipitates. This is the age of racing, because people are always in a hurry these days and I doubt if many know where they are really going. They're burning it up and those of you who speed like lunatics through the fear-filled countryside would be well advised to slow down when you're passing the hallowed entrance to a bohareen. You would be wise to stop and stroll down. The heady scents and peaceful surroundings might steady you down and, who knows, the half-hour you should spend there might not be the cause of saving your life but it could be the cause of saving somebody else's.

I don't know what put bonnets into my head but the setting for a flowery bonnet is a bohareen, a background of browsing cows and woodbine wild.

49

Nobody thinks more of the bohareen than he who has no access to it. Many a man in New York, Durban or London would give his right hand to saunter down the distant bohareens of his boyhood and the woman who wrote the 'Old Bog Road' was one whose heart was in the right place or, if you like, in her native bohareen.

The bohareen is the bye-way of the uncommercial traveller. It is absolutely rustic and the man who pollutes its purity with the exhaust-fumes of an obstreperous motorbike is guilty of sacrilege to say the least. Even bicycles should be barred and nothing but what is truly conservative admitted to its protective windings. A small chuckling stream may accompany it but this is not really necessary either, so long as there is no scarcity of sheltering whitethorns and an adequate disorder of all that is wild in flowers. Nowhere does the bee buzz so soothingly and even the bandit wasp is respectful in such sacred precincts.

Blackberries and elderberries thrive there and it is a poor bohareen that doesn't lead to shining sloe groves and mushroom-dotted pastures. Instead of a gin and tonic I would be inclined to saunter down a bohareen to assuage the pangs of hangovers and sick heads. I have never visited a psychiatrist. Why should I when I can go to a bohareen for nothing and figure myself out at my ease?

You don't need an umbrella or a plastic coat if your choice of walk favours the bohareen. You can stretch yourself back against a mattress-like hedge and relax under a canopy of mixed leaves. The fragrance of crushed herbs will delight you while the rain hammers the open roads and drenches the green fields.

It is rather strange that those who mass-produce attractive picture-postcards should show a somewhat prejudiced preference for ungainly cliffs and unsporting seas. I have never seen a picture postcard depicting a genuine Irish bohareen but still, despite all forms of neglect and the absence of any sort of National Bohareen Protective Society, the tiny unchartered lanes of tousled greenery have lost none of their charm and still remain unspoiled and unobtrusive.

Some time, if you have little else to do when you visit a great city, you may see a prosperous elderly man leaning across the parapet of a birdge. Do not disturb him if you are looking for the nearest way to the theatre. He is remembering evenings of long, long ago and wishing that he was back again walking the bohareens of his green years.

Had I my chance to journey back, or own a King's abode
'Tis soon I'd see the hawthorn tree down the Old Bog Road.

BUTT-SUCKING

Art is a word which I suspect greatly. I suspect it because it confuses and also because nobody has defined it properly or in depth. When I was a boy I took it that art meant painting, but as I grew older I would hear, from time to time, a great variety of people referred to as artistes. Footballers and hurlers qualified for the title. So did dart players and accordion players, not to mention melodeon players. I hope that nobody is under the foolish impression that I am being patronising. Far from it.

I wholeheartedly endorse the terming of the above mentioned people as artistes and the reason I opened in such a vein was to pave the way, as it were, for that which is to follow, to wit; the are of butt-sucking. It is an art which is now largely confined to the poor and the needy, but this does not make it any bit less artistic.

Others who indulge in the art are the young but since these are nearly always poor and needy there is hardly any need to bracket them.

I would not, I assure you, be writing about the art of butt-sucking at all were it not for the fact that the view from my upstairs window impelled me to do so. There I was vainly thinking of something which might contribute to the making of an essay when I noticed a man with a torn over-coat leaning with his back against the wall of a house. He was smoking a cigarette, most of which had been burned and puffed away. What was left was hardly half-an-inch long. In spite of the length he continued to smoke it until it was no longer visible and it seemed that he was smoking his fingers.

Indeed, there was no sign whatsoever of the butt and an innocent bystander might be forgiven if he thought that the man was smoking his fingers. So it would seem, but those of us who smoked in our youth would know otherwise and would be in a position to appreciate the finer points of the efforts our friend was making to prolong the life of the butt.

As he drew on the remains of what was once a proud cigarette his lips protruded like the suckers of a lamprey eel. The muscles on his neck stood out like mountain ranges on a relief map and he was hunched forward like a rugby hooker the better to draw the last breath of life from the infinitesimal weed between his fingers. This man knew his job. If he were a rich man he would have discarded the cigarette at the half way stage, and lighted another. He would not, however, have enjoyed it nearly as as much because hunger is the best sauce and there is nothing as sweet as a cigarette butt when you have not got the means of obtaining more.

As I watched I admired. He reminded me of the not too distant days when I was a butt-sucker myself.

My first attempts to smoke were somewhat abortive but as time passed I found I could smoke with ease and after a while I became an addict. It is not easy to become an addict when money is scarce, and worse still, when everybody else finds money is scarce as well. As a result of this scarcity of money fags were hard to get and one had to be content with butts. There were many others who became so proficient at butt-smoking that it was almost impossible to detect the butts between their fingers.

Often we would be taken aside by well-meaning adults

who would warn us of the dangers of smoking. We would promise that we would never smoke again and all the time there would be a smouldering butt between the fingers, not to mention the fact that the hand which adjoined such fingers was also thrust into a trousers pocket.

We were so proficient that nobody could tell what we were smoking save possibly another butt-sucker. Just because butt-sucking is an art does not mean that it is good. On the contrary, nothing is calculated to speed up a person's departure from this world. Having made myself clear on this point, let me say that the art of butt-sucking which flourished with abandon for so long is now positively on the way out. Affluence is the cause and these days almost everybody throws the cigarette away before it is finished.

Still one comes across the occasional sucker. Almost always he is a poverty-stricken wretch, but nevertheless he serves to remind us that great art can flourish in any climate.

MORNING SOCIALS

Looking out of my window the other morning, I beheld two middle-aged women with message-bags.

The bag of one held cabbage and potatoes. There was also a bloodstained brown-paper parcel which contained either chops, steak, or boiling beef. The message-bag of the other carried cabbage and potatoes also but the meat looked like bacon. The parcel was neater, without bloodstains and it is my belief that there may have been a pound and a half of good quality bacon involved.

The women conversed for some time. The face of one grew serious and perturbed when the other disclosed certain facts. Fingers wagged as much as tongues and the other woman who had been listening took up the running. Time ticked on and the Convent clock struck eleven.

'I'll be killed!' said one, but she made no move to leave.

'They'll be out from school', said the other but instead of departing she launched into another story. There was some laughter, some sighing, some headshaking and there was a marked coolness when a third woman with a message-bag joined them. Here, I told myself, are three people from three separate walks of life. Here, I told myself, are three cooks, three mothers, three wives. Here are three citizens, three voters, three television-viewers. They're all these things, I told myself and yet they're women too. They are engaged in women's conversation. This is hallowed ground and no man may enter.

I ask myself what was so unusual about the little gathering but could not find the answer. A fourth woman joined the party and they talked on. They shifted a little now and then to make way for other pedestrians. They all stopped talking occasionally to acknowledge the salute of a passer-by. They smiled and immediately their faces became serious again as news of import circulated. Further up the street, on the other side, three other women stood in a group. In the distance it could be seen from the nodding of their heads and the eloquence of their hands that news was being swapped. Directly underneath me the talk went on. I could not hear a word of what was being said nor did I want to. I tried to fathom the causes of such conversations and in the end I got it.

These informal street-gatherings are what pubs are to men. These are social get-togethers, unadvertised but not accidental.

Occasionally a phrase did come across, such as: *'They say it cost twenty pounds!'* or *'He don't like it fat!'* One particular phrase which recurred consistently was: *'I'll be killed!'* Each of the women said this from time to time as if it were a ritual. The phrase intrigued me but it was not, I knew, to be taken at face value.

Every woman who participates in the pre-dinner parley is obliged to say it now and then. It means that she is rushing the conversation, that she is afraid enough will not be disclosed in the time left at her disposal. I often heard my own wife say it while she stood in the doorway exchanging views with a friend. When the conversation dragged, she would say: *'I'll be killed!'* I myself the innocent party without malice, not to mind murder, would listen to this and know that the conversation was only beginning.

Beneath me, the four women changed their message-bags from one hand to the other. One put hers on the ground and re-adjusted her headscarf. *'I'll be killed!'* she said and listened eagerly to what another woman was saying.

If I had been truly chivalrous I would have located a tray and sent it into the street with four cups of coffee and a plate of biscuits. I fear, however, that my kindness might be taken for sarcasm and while I do not mind incurring the wrath of my fellows, I draw the line at a gathering of four basking housewives.

Hardly fifteen minutes had elapsed since the meeting had begun. The woman with the cabbage, potatoes, and bacon seemed to be the chairman. Now and then she acknowledged a point of order and gave short shrift to unsubstantiated contributions.

Finally she brought her gavel to bear on the message-bag and concluded the proceedings with the following satisfying summary: *' 'Tis all hours of the morning, I'll be killed!'*

LATCH KEYS

The mature man is always awake to the prospect of calamity.

He recognises, whatever provision he may have made, that the unexpected is always on the horizon and that the price of equanimity is eternal vigilance.

Be that as it may, as the man said, none of us is proof against fate and the wisest among us is the one who oftenest forgets his latch-key. Those of us, and we are many, who have forgotten will appreciate what I will now try to convey. It is only when one arrives at one's own door that the initial search is initiated. One runs through the pockets the first time swiftly and confidently. Then the reality dawns slowly and a second more careful search is carried out. This bears no fruit either and now comes the final excruciating exploration.

One by one articles are taken from the pockets and placed on the ground outside the door. All loose change is first removed because latch-key losers know only too well how difficult it is to locate a key amid a pocketful of coppers and silver pieces. Next comes the handkerchief which is shaken thoroughly lest the key is hidden somewhere in its folds. Then follow the cigarettes, matches and the other odds and ends to which civilised man is a slave. All the pockets are searched again, fruitlessly. All the articles are returned to the pockets and I regret to say there is sometimes profanity. This is a mental rather than a vocal profanity but if one is to judge from the expression on the victim's face some loaded expressions are going the rounds in his head.

There is no point in knocking at the door because most wives are afraid to come downstairs at such an hour. There is also the possibility that she is fast asleep and if she should be awake and hear distant knocking who is to say but it may be on somebody else's door. She may also righteously console herself with the fact that her last words when he left home that evening consisted of a reminder that he should not forget his latch-key. She knows her man and knows that in his excitement to be away he is prone to overlook what he believes to be trivialities. Now, as he stands alone on the deserted street, the folly of his hurry plagues and irritates him.

There is another reason why he may not bang loudly on the door and this is because his neighbours often have better hearing than his wife. They are also, naturally, inquisitive and other wives often derive great satisfaction from the knowledge that somebody else's husband has been out carousing. The satisfaction is all the sweeter when their own husbands are safely in bed.

'Merciful God!' they say, 'he's out again to-night'.

Down below on the quiet street our friend is still going through his pockets, more for the sake of something to do than in the hope of finding anything. Now, if he has a 'phone, things are not so bad. He may go to the nearest kiosk or, if this is impractical, he may go to the barracks where he will be treated with sympathy and understanding. He may even be offered a cup of tea if the time for tea is ripe.

But what if he has no 'phone. Well, now we are faced with a tricky situation. He may knock with a coin on the fanlight in the hope that the missus might be up, attending to the child. As I said, however, knocking is a last resort and he does not want to be the cause of rousing the whole street. Man is at least imaginative and inventive so he goes around to the back of the house and surveys the situation. He girds himself for a climb and quite often he succeeds but, alas and alack, a man who is fortified by strong drink is inclined to over-estimate his athletic capabilities and I have personally known of individuals who broke hands and legs in foolhardy attempts to scale walls or roofs of backhouses.

If he is young and relatively fit, entry will be no problem but those of us who are heavily paunched and woefully unmuscled would be better advised to use the head instead of the limbs.

Here is what I recommend. The backway should be searched thoroughly for empty cannisters. These are easy enough to find as their silvery brightness stands out in the moonlight. When a plentiful supply of these is gathered they should be thrown, one at a time, into the backyard. Nothing – and I repeat, nothing – has the noisome flavour of a night-time canister landing suddenly out of the sky. It rattles, clatters and bangs to an extent which would put larger and more orthodox missiles to shame. If one of these won't wake her then several will. Once awake, she may be called. Do not begin by saying: 'Open up, it's me!' The neighbours derive hilarious moments from statements like this. Just say: 'I forgot my key!' and wait for the step of the saviour. If there is a torrent of abuse, or if there is frosty silence, make no contribution to a situation which has developed very much in your favour. Be grateful to be in out of the night's loneliness and if you have any canisters left throw them into the backyards of your neighbours.

GREAT GOALKEEPERS OF OUR TIME

Monuments are never erected to the type of man I have in mind. His words are never quoted and his opinion rarely sought. His greatest quality is his abundance. He forms the majority. He is ninety-nine per cent of any crowd and you can almost be certain that he will never be interviewed on a television programme. When he dies only a few will mourn him, but that is hardly the point, for this man has made his contribution and that, in itself, is worthy of mention.

But perhaps my picture is not too easily recognisable so I will try to draw the man accurately — and the only way to do that is to create a situation.

First of all, take any given Sunday in summertime. He gets out of bed. He shaves. He dons his sportscoat, flannel pants, and sandals and goes downstairs to a breakfast which inevitably consists of a rasher, an egg and a sausage. He is not feeling too well but he puts the breakfast where it belongs all the same. He glances through the papers and goes to Mass. He doesn't go too far up the Church but he doesn't stand at the door either. After Mass he stands at the nearest corner for a few minutes. He meets a man just like himself. There may be certain physical differences but they are two of a kind. A stranger looking on would be at pains to observe any sort of communication between the two but, by some colossal instinct which defies analysis, they enter a nearby public-house together.

In the public-house the customers are talking about a football match. The local team are playing in a challenge game in a village several miles away. Our man goes home to his dinner of roast beef, peas and potatoes. He has a good stroke with a knife and fork and is no joke when it comes to making the spuds disappear. After dinner he is between two minds — whether to go to bed or take out his bicycle and go to the football match. The stout and the heavy meal have made him drowsy but the instinct of the sportsman is strong within him. An uncle of his was once a substitute for the North Kerry Juniors and a cousin of his mother's was suspended for abusing a referee.

Our hero duly arrives at the football pitch. The crowd is small as this is a game of little consequence. He parks his bicycle and pays a shilling admission fee. The teams are taking the field. His interest is aroused. He gives vent to a spirited yell in support of his own team. The familiar jerseys have brought his loyalty to the surface but he notices a discrepancy in the side. He counts only fourteen men and then, suddenly, he hears his name being called. The first faint suspicion dawns on him but he pretends he doesn't hear. Casually he begins to saunter to the other end of the field but the voice, pursuing him, grows louder. He increases his gait but the unmistakeable call arrests him:

'Hi Patcheen! Will you stand in goals?'

He can run away now and be forever disgraced in the eyes of his neighbours, or he can stand and be disgraced anyway. His coat is whipped off and, before he knows it, there is a jersey being pulled over his head. He hears a disparaging comment from some onlookers on the sideline:

'Good God! Look what they have in goals?'

His blood is up. He thrusts his trousers inside his

socks and tightens his shoelaces. He takes up his position and the game is on.

He is not called upon to do anything during the first half or during the second half either. There is little between the teams but what little there is stands in favour of our man's team. A high lobbing ball drops into the square. The backs keep the forwards at bay and our man goes for the ball. He gets it — only barely but the important thing is that he gets it. The forwards are in on top of him. He's down. He holds on to the ball like a drowning man and for the excellent reason that he has nothing else to hold on to. He hears a rending sound. His flannel trousers are torn. One of the shoes is pulled off his foot. Someone has a hold on his tie and is trying to choke him. He is kicked in the shin and he receives a treacherous wallop in the eye. There must be a hundred men on top of him!

Then the whistle sounds and he is able to breathe freely. He is safe now and here, at last, is his great opportunity. He rises with the ball in his hands. He hops it defiantly and then, in one of those great moments which only happen once in a lifetime, he goes solo-ing down the field. The whistle blows again but he pretends not to hear it. Then he stops and turns and with a tremendous kick aims the ball straight at the referee. Dignified, he returns to his goals with his torn flannels flapping behind him and his tie sticking out from the back of his neck like a pennant on the lance of a crusader.

Nobody offers him a lift after the game. He cycles home to his supper of cold beef and bread and butter. He changes his clothes and makes no attempt to conceal the black eye. He combs his hair and walks down to the corner. He meets his pal and they stroll leisurely towards the public-house.

Our man calls for two pints and, settling himself comfortably on his stool, launches into a detailed account of the save. If he adds a little it is understandable — and if he had been wearing togs and boots heaven only knows what would have happened. The important thing is that he wasn't found wanting when his time came. He made no headlines but he didn't disgrace himself either. The football scribes will not mention him when the annals of the great are being compiled but in the eyes of his compeers and in consideration of the porter he had drunk and of the dinner he had eaten I think he must surely be reckoned among the great goalkeepers of our time.

SIDEWAYS TALKERS

There are certain individuals, male and female, who, for reasons best known to themselves, avert their heads when talking to other people.

This was brought home to me, very forcibly, last week at a social. A number of us were gathered in the bar prior to the table-stakes when a woman addressed me:

'Give me your hankerchief', she said, 'and let no one see you'.

I dearly love mysteries so, without more ado, I produced a spotless white hankerchief, looked carefully around to see if I was being observed and thrust it swiftly into her hand. Her reaction was as though I had slapped her. She let my hankerchief fall to the ground without a word of thanks and accepted another, not half as clean, from a stout gentleman who stood at her other side. I stopped to retrieve my hankerchief and, as I did, I distinctly heard her say: 'the cheek of some people!'

I put my hankerchief back into my pocket, drew the barmaid's attention and called for a drink for myself and a friend who happened to be with me. Conversation proceeded all round me with a nice lively hum and it was plain to see that everybody was having a good time. Then, quite unexpectedly, the woman who asked me for the hankerchief turned towards me and, without looking at me directly, said: 'You'll have one on me!'

Well, I thought, she's not too bad after all. She's trying to make it up to me.

'No, thank you!' I said. 'I'd rather not, but I appreciate it just the same'.

'Merciful God!' she said aloud, 'there's a fellow here off his rocker'.

It was only then that it dawned on me that the woman was a sideways talker, that is to say, when she spoke, she never addressed herself directly to the person in question.

After that I ignored her, although it seemed from time to time that she was talking to me and I almost replied when, on one occasion, she said: 'Don't go in for the duckling or you'll be rumbling all night!' I was going to say that duckling never affected me in this fashion but I guessed, quite rightly, that she was advising the gentleman on the other side of her. Just then a young chap, with a white short coat, appeared on the scene and told us all confidentially that the meal was ready if we were.

On the way I brushed shoulders with the gentleman whose hankerchief the lady had accepted.

'Pull back a minute', he said.

I did so and the rest of the crowd passed by on their way to the table.

'I supose', said he, 'you thought my wife was talking to you?'

'I certainly did!' I told him.

'It happens all the time', he said. 'As a matter of fact when I proposed to her we were sitting in the balcony of a dancehall. I was sitting on her left side but unfortunately there was another man sitting, half-asleep, on her right. I took the bull by the horns and popped the question.

' "I'll marry you", she said, "if you give up the

motor-bike because I don't want to be a widow early".

' "Faith, you won't!" said the man on the other side, "because I'm married already and, besides, I'm a hackney driver".'

I cluck-clucked sympathetically.

'That was all right', said my friend, 'if 'twas let go at that, but what did she do then?'

'I don't know!' I told him truthfully.

'She turned around and gave the unfortunate man a slap across the face. You see, these people who talk sideways are certain they are talking straight. For instance to-night when she spoke to you, as it seemed, nothing would convince her but that she had spoken to me'.

'What did the hackney-driver do?' I asked.

'He got up and offered me out to fight so I got up and went out with him but at the door I explained my case to him we parted on good terms'.

The husband of the woman who talked sideways went to join her and I took my place with my friend at the far end of the table.

The soup arrived and the course passed pleasantly. The fish arrived and it was during the middle of this course that the commotion began. It was, of course, the woman who talked sideways. She was speaking in a loud angry voice while two waiters, one with a long blue coat and one with a short white one, endeavoured to mollify her. Her husband, cutely enough, quit the scene quickly on some pretext or other and headed directly for the bar. Curiosity prompted me to follow him.

'Well?' I asked, 'what happened?'

'It's like this', he said. 'When the fish arrived she complained to the waiter that there wasn't enough sauce on it. Then she turned to me and asked me to pour salad cream on it for her. I did as she bade but so did the man who sat next to her and so did both waiters with the result that her plate is now overflowing with salad cream and she can't find the fish'.

'You're a martyr!' I told him.

'I know', he said.

'What will you do now?' I asked him.

'Nothing!' he said. 'I'll go back and join her as soon as she finished my fish'.

THE SPIRIT OF CHRISTMAS

Many years ago on our street in Ireland there lived an old woman who had but one son whose name was Jack. Jack's father had died when Jack was no more than a gorsoon but Jack's mother went out and worked to support her son and herself. As Jack grew older she stil went out and worked for the good reason that Jack did not like work. The people in the street used to say that Jack was only good for three things. He was good for eating. He was good for smoking and he was good for drinking.

To give him his due he never beat his mother or kicked her. All he did was to skedaddle to England when she was too old to go out and work. Years passed but she never had a line from her only son. Every Christmas she would stand inside her window waiting for a card or a letter. She waited in vain.

When Christmas came to our street it came with a loud laugh and an expansive humour that healed old sores and lifted the hearts of young and old. If the Christmas that came to our street were a person he would be something like this. He would be in his sixties but glowing with rude health. His face would be flushed and chubby with sideburns to the rims of his jaws. He would be wearing gaiters and a tweed suit and he would be mildly intoxicated. His pockets would be filled with silver for small boys and girls, and for the older folk he would have a party at which he would preside with his waistcoat paunch extending benignly and his posterior benefiting from the glow of a roaring log fire. There would be scalding punch for everybody and there would be roast geese and ducks, their beautiful golden symmetries exposed on large dishes and tantalizing jobs of potato stuffing oozing and bursting from their hip pockets.

There would be singing and storytelling and laughter and perhaps a tear here and there when absent friends were toasted. There would be gifts for everybody and there would be great goodwill as neighbours embraced each other, promising to cherish each other till another twelve-month had passed.

But Christmas is an occasion and not a person. A person can do things, change things, create things, but all our occasions are only what we want them to be. For this reason Jack's mother waited, Christmas after Christmas, for word of her wandering boy. To other houses would come stout registered envelopes from distant loved ones who remembered. There would be bristling, crumply-envelopes from America with noble, rectangular cheques to delight the eye and comfort the soul.

There would be parcels and packages of all shapes and sizes so that every house became a warehouse until the great day came when all the goods would be distributed.

Now it happened that in our street there was a postman who knew a lot more about his customers than they knew about themselves.

When Christmas came he was weighted with bags of letters and parcels. People awaited his arrival the way children await a bishop on confirmation day. He was not averse to indulging in a drop of the comforts wherever such comforts were tendered. But comforts or no comforts the man was no fool.

When he came to the house where the old woman lived he would crawl on all fours past the window. He just hadn't the heart to go by and be seen. He hated to disappoint people, particularly old people. For the whole week before Christmas she would take up her position behind the faded curtains waiting for the letter which never came.

Finally the postman could bear it no longer. On Christmas Eve he delivered to our house a mixed bunch of cards and letters. Some were from England. He requested one of these envelopes when its contents were removed. He re-wrote the name and address and also he wrote a short note which he signed 'your loving son Jack'. Then from his pocket he extracted two pounds which he placed in the envelope. There was no fear the old woman would notice the handwriting because if Jack was good at some things as I have already mentioned he was not good at other things and one of these was writing. In fact he could not write his name.

When he came to the old woman's door he knocked loudly. When she appeared he put on his best official voice and said 'Sign for this if you please, missus'. The old woman signed and opened the envelope. The tears appeared in her eyes and she cried out loud, 'I declare to God Jack is a scholar'. 'True for you', said the postman, ' and I dare say he couldn't get in touch with you till he learned how to write'.

'I always knew there was good in him', she cried, 'I always knew it'.

'There was good in everyone, missus', said the postman as he moved on to the next house.

The street was not slow in getting the message and in the next and last post there were many parcels for the old woman. It was probably the best Christmas the street ever had.

BOASTING

Boasting is not as common as it used to be, or maybe 'tis how people have grown cuter at it!

False modesty is as effective a method of boasting as any and, if the part is acted well, the most impressive claims can be established.

The day is gone forever when men went around with Junior football medals on their lapels. A Junior football medal or a step-dancing medal was as important as hair-oil or a tiepin when I first started going to dances. They were all in the same class as letters of introduction and girls nearly always asked what the medals were for.

However, the best method of boasting, when I was younger, was boasting through the medium of a second party. This party should be a close acquaintance, familiar with the history of his subject. I had such a friend in my youth and as he did unto me I did unto him. There was a certain red-haired girl with whom he was greatly taken for a short period but all his efforts to date her had failed. Dancing with her one night I mentioned my friend's name.

'Yerra, don't mind that fella!' she said.

'He saved a man from drowning once', I told her.

She immediately showed some interest. 'Did he get anything for it?' she asked.

'No!' I said cheerfully. 'He dashed off without telling anybody who he was'.

Thereafter she eyed him all night but he was so flattered that he ignored her.

In our street, when I was a small boy, there was a certain unfortunate family. This type of family is to be found in every street and in every community and, according to themselves, they always possess more and know more than their neighbours. Children would come home to their parents with the depressing news that Mickey So-and-So's daddy had more money than their own daddy or that Mary So-and-So's mother had all sorts of jewellery, more jewellery than the rest of the women in the street put together. First Communions came and their frocks, naturally, were dearer than other frocks. All of us young ones were stymied whenever we were boastfully asked the attainments of parents or relatives. We were always outclassed but one day a small boy finished their boasting for ever when one of these intolerable know-alls announced that his daddy was once in America. We all gasped at this because we knew that in our wildest dreams this claim could not be surpassed. Suddenly the small boy in question chipped in:

'Your father was never in jail', he said, 'the same as my father!'

This gave us great heart and a small girl said: 'or your father isn't as dirty as my father!'

A third party spoke up and clinched it: 'Your father was never as drunk as my father!' she announced.

The know-alls and have-alls were disarranged and dumbdazzled. They fled home in disorder and emerged later the most chastened and agreeable of children.

I knew another man who occupied a high rung on the community ladder by virtue of the attainments of his brother. We might be seated, a crowd of us, in a publichouse or outside our doors when the discussion would range from local to foreign affairs.

'That was an awful bloodbath in Nigeria!' someone

would comment.

Our friend, whom I will call Jack since it is as good a name as any other, would purse his lips at this and look quite solemn.

'It must be a holy terror in Nigeria now', would come a second comment.

'They aren't half as bad as they're painted', Jack would say nonchalantly.

'Ah, come off it!' we would all say.

' 'Tis true!' Jack would reply. 'The brother was often there and he says they're the same as ourselves when you get to know them!'

Or we might be discussing a world title fight and Billy Conn would be the man under discussion.

'His mother is Irish!' Jack would announce.

'Indeed she's not!' we would reply immediately. 'Why don't you read the papers, man?'

'Don't mind the papers', Jack would say with an unshakable air of authority. 'His mother is a native of Templeglantine'.

'Where in blazes did you see that?' we would ask indignantly.

But Jack was master of the situation. 'I saw it nowhere', he would say calmly. 'I'm only telling you what the brother told me. Himself and Billy were in the same digs for two years, slept in the same bed and ate off the same table and if the brother don't know will you kindly tell me who does!'

There was no answer to this and Jack remained unassailable. No one ever saw Jack's brother and no one knew how he communicated with Jack. He had been gone for twenty years and since nobody remembered him he was a legendary figure.

Time passed and a new Pope was elected. It had come over the radio that white smoke had risen from the Vatican chimney. We all expressed wonder since nobody expected that the candidate in question would be elected.

'I knew it last night!' said Jack.

We scoffed at this and indeed some of us laughed.

'Where there's smoke there's fire!' said Jack.

'We know that!' we shouted.

'Yes', said Jack unperturbed. 'But who do you think was in charge of the fire?'

'The brother!' we all shouted.

'No!' said Jack, 'the sister!'

PADDLING

The reason I write about paddling at all is that the season for it has just begun. Unfortunately, however, it would seem to be losing ground in the field of outdoor activities. The dedicated paddler is a cross between a landlubber and a sailor and paddling itself is a pastime which might be described as beneficial and stimulating.

Now, for many years, although not a full-time paddler, I have made a study of paddling and paddlers and I have come to the conclusion that the most enthusiastic and unrelenting of all paddlers is your elderly lady. For a while I contemplated a short book which I decided to call 'The Complete Paddler' or 'The Art of Paddling' but I abandoned the idea as it might have a perverse effect on paddling.

The male paddler is, for the most part, elderly and although the toddler may seem to be more abundant in seaside resorts he is no more than a splasher. Besides, paddling in a bathing suit is against all the rules.

The senior male paddler is an interesting study.

He is quick-tempered and short-winded and he paddles with his neck arched forward like a swan as if he were admiring his toes in the water. He begins by taking off his shoes, never his hat. This is followed by the removal of socks and, finally, collar and tie. In passing, it might be no harm to mention that it is almost sacrilegeous to paddle while wearing a collar and tie. Hats and caps are permissible. Indeed they are the *sine qua non* of all qualified paddlers for, while one can easily see the dangers lurking below, one can never be sure of what will come from above. Having removed the aforementioned garments the male paddler pulls his hat or cap firmly on his head. He rolls up his trousers above the knees, often exhibiting knotty calves and bunion-cluttered feet. He does not care if the purple traceries of his varicose veins attract curiosity. He then places his hands in his trousers pockets, extends his paunch and saunters seawards. He steps into the water without testing its temperature and savours its salving but at once salt-laden stings. If he were a seal or a dog he would bark. It would be a deep growl of supreme satisfaction. It is dangerous to disturb him in this, the early stage of his ritual. He bends downwards, grunting like an all-in wrestler and separates one toe from another until all could be described as having achieved temporary independence.

He then walks in a line parallel with the beach, at a depth of nine inches, looking neither to left nor to right. He dislikes noisy swimmers. He does not like to get splashed and may sometimes remonstrate when dippers cross his bows. When in a semi-bibulous mood he is not above drawing a kick or a clout at those who would encroach upon his preserves.

The elderly female, on the other hand, is a more sedate, more unruffled and a far more happy paddler. She is tolerant of those who occupy the sea and it is conceiveable that she may be reciting one of her many novenas as she moves slowly and imperturbably with the ponderous grace of a great sailing ship. The front of her skirt or dress is held in her right hand the way a nervous opera-singer might clutch a silk handerchief. She smiles at all and sundry, stops to nod at small boys and girls, looks about her betimes to admire the lay of the land and is not above the odd playful kick when

77

she feels that nobody is watching her.

There are, of course, several other kinds of paddlers but the above are the chief ones or what the ornithologist might describe as 'the greater greyhaired wrinkle-crested paddler'.

I have little experience of other types and perhaps am not qualified to investigate them closely and with detachment. One of the earliest paddles I remember was conducted by a female relation of my mother's. I was very small at the time and we were walking along the beach hand in hand minding our own business. She was about twenty and she was the first to notice that a man was following us. She said it as if she disaproved but from her face one might safely gather that she was markedly excited. He passed us back and forth several times after that and endeavoured to attract her attention with a variety of salutes and grimaces of which any actor might be proud. Finally, he approached and asked if she would care for a paddle. He wasn't a bad-looking chap.

'All right', she said 'but you'll have to take the child by the hand'.

I dared to presume that they were not unacquainted.

The ultimate upshot of that particular paddle was that now the pair are happily married with as fine a family of paddlers as ever dipped toes in salt water.

WATERY EYES

People who wear lonely faces are not necessarily lonesome people. Much the same applies to people who have watery eyes. We tend to think that these are teary eyes. The truth is that tears and eye-water come from two different fountains. Do not ask me where these fountains are situated. All I can tell you is that they are in the neighbourhood of the noodle. Go to your doctor if you want exact information but don't tell him I sent you.

Watery eyes are just about the most priceless possession a man or woman can have in this little globular demesne of ours. Since, unfortunately, it is a demesne where hypocrisy is more abundant than charity watery eyes can be greatly undervalued by those who are lucky enough to possess them. I myself do not possess watery eyes except when there is a strong wind blowing into my face or on rarer occasions when I am the victim of a head cold.

My ancestors, however, were not deficient in the matter of eye-water and there was one particularly vicious relative who had a good word for nobody but who was greatly liked and respected by his neighbours. They said that in spite of his scurrilous tongue he had great nature. Nature, in those days, was a thing no sensible man should be without. A man with nature, whatever else he might not have, was always accorded respect and if ever his neighbours were heard to criticise him someone was always quick to point out that for all his faults he had great nature. This generally nipped the criticism in the bud.

Anyway this relative of mine was a great man for attending funerals. The only reason he went to funerals was to pass away the time. He did not like plays or pictures and besides you had to pay good money before you were left inside the door of a playhouse or cinema. Funerals cost nothing and he never failed to express his delight when he heard somebody was dead. He had as little time for the dead as he had for the living. Ordinary people who were fond of criticising a deceased party when he was alive always stopped the practice when he was pronounced dead.

There were two reasons for this. A dead man was harmless and therefore praise couldn't do him any good. Number two the louder the praise given at the dead man's wake the greater the quantity of strong drink given to the bestower of the praise.

But to get back to my relative. On the morning of the funeral he would shave and dress in his Sunday best. Always he would make his way to the front of the funeral where he would be seen by all the relatives of the deceased. He always walked with his head well bent and his hands behind his back. This sort of posture impressed everybody.

At the gate of the churchyard he would precede the coffin party to the grave and stand watching all those who came to pay their respects. Those who did not know him often mistook him for a detective.

At the graveside his eyes would begin to water. He could not keep it back and it often ran down the side of his face. He would produce his hankerchief and blow his nose. Then he would wipe the water away. I once heard a woman behind me say to another: 'God bless that man but he has woeful nature'.

As the water coursed down his face others who were at the graveside, particularly middle-aged women who were in no way related to the dead man, would sniff at the sight of him. These sniffs were the harbingers of genuine salt tears. They would look at my relative again, and believing him to be genuinely crying, would start off themselves. Soon every woman at the graveside was crying. They could not stop even if they had wanted to. Handkerchiefs appeared by the score and eyes were dried only to fill again from the inexhaustible well of tears owned by every woman. If there was a fresh breeze his eyes would really swim and very often sympathetic souls would come forward and place the hand of consolation on his shoulder.

When he died he had a large funeral. It was dominated by women. All had a plentiful supply of handkerchiefs but they were never called upon to use them. Not a tear was shed because they had nobody to lead them. Their tear-leader was no more and he who was the cause of so many was buried without a single tear in the end.

THE MOUSE'S RETURN

Any day now the first winter snows will whiten the mountain-tops and from the North the geese will come in long-barbed arrowheads. Now toes grow numb while fingertips are chilled. Already long noses redden in the winter wind and ears are nibbled by the searching frost.

'You can expect him back any day now!' I told the misses, 'his wanderings are over and his heels need cocking up'.

None of us knew where he had gone since mice do not migrate but he was missing and there was no question about that. The girl who works for us hadn't screeched for weeks and the rest of the household were sure that he had taken the poisoned meal which I was supposed to have spread for him. But I hadn't spread the meal and I was in the know! I suspected for long that he was an adventurous soul who wanted to see beyond the horizon, for mice like men are subject to wanderlust but the cold sends them scurrying home along leaf-covered lanes and frosty mouse-paths.

'That's the last we'll see of him', everybody said when his chirpings had long faded and his scratchings no longer irritated the womenfolk. I wasn't so sure that he had gone for good. In fact, deep down, I was certain of it for this mouse was nobody's fool and he knew a cushy berth when he spotted one. In addition he was a night mouse and for this he was to be forgiven much. He had accustomed himself to the tantrums of women who make war on mice and pamper the vainest of cats. He knew who his friends were and he only appeared in public when all were abed. He chose to ignore yours truly. No — he didn't truly ignore me. He took me for granted and went about his business as if I wasn't there at all. Whenever I shifted a foot or lighted a cigarette he would pause cautiously, but only for an instant. He knew my ways and there existed between us the nodding acquaintance of suburban neighbours who do not want to know each other better but who are happy to exchange civil 'good-mornings' and pleasant 'good-nights'. There was mutual respect but none of that familiar, back-slapping intimacy which is born overnight and which never stands the test of time.

Anyway, you will be glad to hear he is back and with him he has brought a friend, who I suspect is female. They never go out of doors together, just one at a time, so I'll leave you to draw your own conclusions in this respect.

He returned from his exile at two o'clock on Saturday morning last. I placed my pencil behind my ear and smiled when I heard his first excited chirping. He is a ventriloquist, I told myself, or he has taken a mate. I was anxious to see the mother of his family for in a way I felt responsible for him. She was not as daring as he for he had the guts to come within six feet of me, there to stare at me unblinkingly while she merely thrust herself flittingly around a corner and disappeared when her eyes caught mine.

In all fairness to him, he had chosen well. She was neither brash nor noisy. If anything she was demure and shy and I haven't seen her since. I suspect that that one fleeting glimpse was in the nature of an introduction.

'That rat that used to be here is back!' the girl said

when she came in from Mass on Sunday morning.

'There are no rats in the house', I told her somewhat coldly.

'Well, whatever it is', she said, 'it's back, because the night light is nibbled and the corner of the margarine is bitten'.

'That', I told her, 'is an itinerant mouse who merely spent a night. He's packed his traps by now and is half way to Abbeyfeale'.

I could see she did not believe me.

'Why should he go to Abbeyfeale', the missus said, 'when he has sympathisers right here?'

'That's right!' said the girl. 'If I was a mouse I'd know where to come. We'll have every mouse in the country here soon'.

The nights passed and life went on. More mice-powder had been laid but my friend and his wife were wise to its dangers. They lived harmoniously together for three nights and then on the fourth the chinking and the squeaking was different and there was rancour and bitterness in the exchanges. One chirp borrowed another and soon they were at it hammer and tongs. It lasted a good while and then there was silence. I suspect they had let off sufficient steam and would, at any moment, make it up. I was right for presently there was the most amiable and conciliatory of chirping and thereafter all was well. There followed two more nights of peace and again there was a row. But after this one I could only distinguish one voice chirping. It was that of my friend. His mate had gone, no doubt to be consoled by her mother.

Mice can be as foolish as humans for what two have broken only two can make up and all the mothers in the world will not mend broken hearts. My friend became disconsolate and moody after that. He broke his bond and took to appearing in the day time. He narrowly missed death from a hunting cat. Cups and saucers were thrown at him and he was twice nearly maimed by a brush-head. Many of us must know how he felt.

At the moment all is well for his beloved has returned to him and now there is harmony where there was bickering. I hope they have learned their lesson as it is I who will have to shoulder the blame. The girl is convinced that I am the party who brought them together again.

NOSES

I am blessed with a long, crooked nose, and to enhance its natural beauty it is a nose which was twice broken and once fractured.

It is a nose which has adapted itself well to varying psychological climates and I must be forgiven if I say that, despite its unattractive angles, I would not part with it for the world. I may eventually will it to some nose hospital if, like Barkis, they are willing.

Most notorious men had long noses — Julius Caesar, Napoleon, Cochise, De Gaulle, and Jimmy Durante, to mention but a few. No disparagement of pug noses or aquiline noses is intended since all noses are prepossessing to their owners. This is as it should be, because if a man doesn't stick up for his own nose, nobody else will. What might seem like an ugly and ill-made proboscis to a total stranger may be an object of disarming beauty to its proprietor.

The nose is an extremely sensitive organ. A clout on the nose is always more effective than a clout in the jaw or the solar plexus. The nose is very near the brain for one thing and a careful wallop on its point can contain a great symbolic element. The nose is the door-knocker of man's tear-fountain and a ringing rap will always result in tears. In addition to bringing tears it dazzles the unfortunate fellow at the receiving end so that he is more inclined to rub the abused area than to protect it. The nose is the Achilles Heel of courageous schoolboys and a promising wrangle was often ended prematurely because of a lucky belt on its extremities.

Some noses achieve colossal sizes and dominate otherwise engaging facial structures to such an extent that it is the nose and not the face that catches the eye. Whiskey and rum have had a big say in the development of what we loosely term the alcoholic nose. This type of nose is nearly always of a deep purple hue with tributary-like veins which stretch out like a railway network in a survey map.

Young ladies are forever making war on shiny noses with powder-puffs, encouraged no doubt by the unfounded belief that a shiny nose is no addition to a glamorous face. I fail to see anything improper or humiliating about shiny noses and it is a wise woman who does not tamper with what is both vivid and natural.

Some noses are permanently red and always look as if they were just after being blown while other noses are always blue. Noses of this type on pale faces result in rather incongruous but nevertheless original colour schemes. Weather is the most important factor in nose colouring and Jack Frost is the artist who achieves most in totally changing the natural hue.

Reference to noses is sometimes hurtful to people who have not been exposed to the vicissitudes of life. That is why I will make no mention of warts or pimples and anyway these are transient features for to-day's pimple may be to-morow's carbuncle. People with extremely small noses need not be so proud. Small noses are a poor foundation for spectacles and pince-nez. Small noses do not make for big thinkers since deep thought is impossible without considerable tapping and pulling of nose-points.

In my youth my own nose was often referred to in

somewhat scathing terms by those who hold that long noses are diverting and conspicious. A man's nose, however, is his own and is cast to match the face that wears it. Take it off and put it on another man's face and the effect will be ludicrous. Medical science will inevitably come up with a relatively safe method of swapping noses but it is a fool who would part with his own nose for a nose he knows nothing whatsoever about. Even at this present time noses can be altered and one wonders if this is for the best. Minor alterations may be necessary in many cases and might serve to enhance the face but a complete change is not advisable for when the nose and the face are independent of each other conflict cannot be avoided.

Nose-blowing is a practice, or rather an art, which is seriously on the decline. It was once a powerful emotional release and a safe retreat when one was embarrassed or unsettled by the unexpected. A man covered his nose and a large part of his face in his handkerchief and the ensuing discord was always intimidating. A loud blow into one's handkerchief at the right moment can be most unnerving. Students of debate would do well to remember this. It can be especially devastating when a member of the opposing team is in the middle of an important sentence. Apart from the jarring effect of the unheralded intrusion it will also drown out the clinching point of his argument and leave him ill-tempered and uncertain.

A crooked nose does not suggest a crooked man and it is my opinion that the more unwieldy the nose the richer the blood that colours it and the stauncher the heart that regulates it.

KNIVES

Recently I followed, with the keenest interest, an exciting bout of correspondence in the evening newspapers. I call it exciting because it had to do with knives. I do not refer to the flick-knife, third hand of the coward nor the dagger not indeed to the knife as a weapon.

The correspondence had to do with the common dinner-knife and, believe me, dinner-knives are exciting when heard with the mixed foursome of spoons, soup spoons, dessert spoons and forks. At least I find them exciting for when I hear their music I know that a meal is being prepared for somebody.

However, to get on with it, some of the participants in the newspaper correspondence unflinchingly condemned the use of the dinner-knife as a vehicle licensed to transport meat from plate to mouth. This, they said, was the function of the fork.

Others said that country people should be excused the habit of using the knife as a meat conveyor. One outraged correspondent referred to the practice as appalling while another denounced it as coarse and vulgar.

I always like to take a stand in matters of this nature although when one is personally involved one is inclined to be blinded to realities, realities which are at once obvious to the detached observer.

You may ask how one can convey gravy with a knife? I will answer that one by asking how can one carry gravy with a fork? If anything, the fork was designed to let gravy escape through its prong-divided head whereas the knife, which is a solid and undivided piece of machinery, can carry small cargoes of gravy or sauce without danger to the person.

Many years ago some scoundrel devised a new method of eating. I do not use the word 'scoundrel' lightly. He introduced us to that pompous and conceited ruffian, the fish-knife. He cluttered our tables with dessert-spoons and several varieties of knives and forks. The majority followed him but some, like myself, did not.

I will eat any way I choose. I will scoop up meat or gravy with my knife or whatever is most convenient. I will forgive those of slavish temperament who look about them sheepishly in case they may be using the wrong instruments. No blame to them for to-day's dinner table is as instrument-laden as the tray of a hospital surgeon.

I remember, when I was a small boy at school, a little woman used to come around every so often and tell us how to eat. She had a little poem which I still remember:

> Monkeys when they sit at table
> Eat up fast as they are able
> Scoop up gravy with their knives
> And gobble for their very lives.

We are all monkeys, I daresay, one way or another and it is good to be reminded of it.

Our teacher had it hot and heavy with the little woman. Like myself he was a knife man who thought for himself and who refused to be influenced by the infantile habits of so-called aristocrats. There was, at the time, in the class a small boy noted for his economy of words and phrases.

He was a lad who could always give a brief but telling summary of events and ideas. He got on well in the world and is now, I am told, a parish clerk in Nebraska with a part-time job at night in one of the most respectable publichouses in Omaha.

One of his statements I will long remember:

'Knives', he said, 'is for eating meat and saucers is for cooling your tea'.

But to go on.

The eating habits of civilised man are the concern of every civilised man and there certainly is a problem as to the methods employed. It is, however, a problem which every man must solve for himself. I am happy to say that I have solved this problem personally and I would like to pass on a few simple rules which my readers may care to follow:

(1) Never be ashamed to use a knife to scoop up gravy if you feel inclined to do so.
(2) Always remember that fish-knives are dagoes, i.e. half-knives.
(3) Make allowances for people who frown on knives as food-conveyors.
(4) Never turn the edgy side of your knife towards your mouth.

I hope these pieces of advice will be of help to my readers, particularly those of tender years.

A DEAR NEIGHBOUR

Many years ago there lived in our community a woman who liked to get her own back on the neighbours by teaching manners to their children whenever an opportunity presented itself. Incidentally, the fact that I so often refer to the chief characteristic of and to the folk who inhabit our community does not mean that it is different in any way from any other community. It is just that it is the terrain which is most familiar to me and because of the fact that asses and mules, stronger animals than I, have gone bogging when in strange territory I think it all the more important that I should stay where I belong.

But let us forge ahead and enlighten the dear student. As I said this woman liked to teach manners to the children of the neighbourhood. To teach them manners, however, she had first to capture them. It was not enough to ask them to take on run-of-the-mill errands. They knew that she was anything but a pleasant character and if she wanted to get one of them into the house the contract would have to be unusual and attractive.

One day she induced a friend of mine to climb up to her chimney where it was obvious that a crow had built himself a temporary dwelling in the foolish hope that winter would never come and that he would be safe and secure in his chimney stronghold all the year round.

But for the possibility of the brush with the crow my friend would never have entered the house. As things turned out he succeeded in evicting the unfortunate bird although it took quite a long while and on two occasions he very nearly fell from the chimney.

When he finally descended he was given soap and water with which he was expected to remove all traces of the combat. He performed this unpleasant task and then stood with his hands behind his back waiting for his payment. There was none forthcoming, at least there was none of the financial kind. She said to him instead 'I have something nice for you'.

She then told him to be seated at the head of the table. He was too much afraid of her to do otherwise. In front of him she placed half a grapefruit.

'You can start off with that', she said. She stood by with her hands folded waiting for him to begin.

'Ma'm', he said, 'I can't eat it'.

She drew in her breath sharply as if it was just what she expected.

'You mean', she laughed, 'you don't know how to eat it'.

To this my friend had no answer. He just sat there with his head down and his eyes averted from the woman. She stood gloating nearby shaking her head now and then at the enormity of the boy's backwardness. These were her moments of glory and she savoured them to the fullest. After all it might be weeks before she came into possession of another boy. My turn to dine in her kitchen came sooner than I expected. Some member of my family received good marks in an exam and the community were proud of the fact. Not so our friend.

She called me one day while I was playing in the street. I was reluctant to answer but she called again more imperiously and I approached her cautiously.

'Will you do a bit of a job for me?' she asked.

'What kind of a job?' I asked suspiciously.

' 'Tis nothing much', she replied, 'only to paint a few chairs'.

At home I was never allowed near either a paint brush or a pot of paint. This was too good an opportunity to be missed. She led me to a shed in the back where two chairs awaited me. I fell to work with a will. In an hour or so I had finished.

'Come in', she said, 'I have your dinner ready'. This was what I feared.

'They'll be expecting me home', I told her.

' 'Tis on the table', she said. She made me sit at the table facing a plate of fish the likes of which I had never seen before. Up to that the only sea fish I had eaten were mackerel and herrings. I was taking no chances. I refused to touch it. With great satisfaction she folded her arms.

'I suppose', she said, 'that's the kind of fish you does have at home'.

'Oh yes', I lied, 'the exact same'. When I refused to eat she smirked. I know now that the fish was plaice. She stood for several minutes gloating and then she told me to go home.

Maybe we had boasted too much about the good marks. It's a known fact that there is nothing but sympathy for those who get bad marks.

GOOD NEWS

I remember, as if it were yesterday, a female neighbour who knew more about our business than she did about her own. I do not hold this against her. Indeed, I commend her for it as I firmly believe that no family should be absolved from frequent inspection by outside observers. It is good both for the family and for the observers and if neither side is satisfied as a result it is well to remember that nobody is above reproach. But where was I? Ah, yes!

This female neighbour was not a bad oul' skin at heart. When you were down she wouldn't dance on you and to give her nothing but her honest due she never reneged on an underdog regardless of his nationality or religious persuasion. It was this that endeared her to one and all.

Like all women and indeed like all men she was not entirely free of fault. She never overlooked her religious duties and if there was a collection for the black babies or the Propagation of the Faith her name was always near the top of the list. To pass a blind or a lame beggar would, in her eyes, be unthinkable. To give offence to those of lesser means or lesser station would be unforgivable. It was often said of her that she would give you the bite she'd be eating, that is to say if you had the stomach for it.

What then was the creature's fault? I'll tell you. She could not and would not accept and under no circumstance be 'party to' or 'agent for' the reception of good news. For instance if her best friend got an account of increased fortune or a win on the sweep or anything whatever that improved the outlook she deserted that best friend at once and never looked at her again until all the fortune was squandered.

In other words she was with you only when you were down or, if you like, she was with you only when you were equal to her or below her but never when you were above her. In this respect she was like most neighbours. You are acceptable only as long as you remain like them. Fall behind them by all means but if you forge ahead you have committed the unforgivable sin of outstripping the field. In their eyes you have then left the fold.

But to return to our friend. In illness it must be said of her that she was as constant in her ministrations as the Northern star. I recall a case in point which may be of some future use to the student.

In the street it was winter. That is to say it was cold and windy and no place for a man in bathing togs. Anyhow as I said earlier it was winter and the old corpsemaker Death was hovering in desolate places waiting to do his work. A number of elderly people were swept away and these were no great loss and it was generally taken for granted that if they didn't go during that particular winter they would go for sure the next one.

As the cold intensified funerals became common-place. Since I never like to write about things which are too common I will not dwell to much on death.

People passed on and others grew ill. One of the latter was a middle-aged woman who lived alone. There wasn't much hope for her and there was talk of shifting her to hospital but then the neighbour who hated good news intervened and volunteered to nurse the patient.

Night and day she sat by the bedside of the sick woman leaving the sickroom only to heat broth or look out the door to see if anybody else was dying.

The days passed and there was no change in the state of the parties. Eventually the woman who hated good news or rather good news relating to others became ill herself and collapsed while attending to her duties. She was carted away to a hospital. Her patient was carted away likewise.

Time passed and the nip began to leave the air. A number of enterprising daffodils appeared out of doors. Blackbird and thrush sang cheerily.

In other words, it was Spring. The woman who hated good news was on her feet and doing well. The woman who brought about her collapse was also doing well. So well was she doing that she ventured out to Mass wearing a new fur coat which had been mailed to her from America by a Monsignor who was a relation to her. When the woman who hated good news saw her through her front window she reddened with ire. After reddening she thought of the injustice of it all. Here was this fur-coated monster alive and well when she should be as dead as mutton. The woman who hated good news collapsed and passed on. What else could she do under the circumstances?

CAT-CALLS

The other night my slumber was disturbed by a congregation of yodelling tom-cats

It began with the insidious bleating of a lonely female and soon from all quarters of the locality came the assertive wailing of innumerable tom-cats. There was nothing to indicate their approach, no flurry of paws, no muffled pouncing but when they arrived they sang together like a crowd of drunken mourners at an old-time wake.

At the back of my house there is a large shed with a flat, corrugated-iron roof and here is the palace of revels. For a while, as if by agreement, there was no sound. Then, in incredible undertone, the she-cat commenced her homily. I have always been amused by people who, when imitating cat-calls, can do no better than the unimaginative meow. To listen to this she-cat, one would think it was a human who addressed her admirers. She began, as do all great orators, in the most casual fashion but slowly her tone heightened and she spoke with unearthly sincerity while the alabaster-like tom-cats ranged round listened attentively. In the dark their eyes shone but not a move was made nor did the vainest of that feline throng lift a paw to scratch or eject a tongue to lick. The female covered a wide range of topics but to the unitiated it must have sounded like the dismal wailing of a banshee whose victim has been unexpectedly cured by aureomycin.

The she-cat plaintively rebuked her audience in the

beginning. She complained of neighbourhood dogs who needed chastising and she went on to stress the dangers of complacency when a new greyhound is introduced to the locality. She cried out loud that her posterior was still sore from some well-placed pellets out of an unlicensed air-gun. She wailed over departed kittens and concluded by praising everybody present but openly showed favour to none. When she had finished there was no sign of approbation. There was total silence. Down the back-lane came the unmistakable clip-clop of an ass with a loose shoe. No cat went to investigate and the sounds faded into the night.

All were agreed that she had spoken wisely if, perhaps, a little too long. Overhead the stars shone like marquisite in the great brooch of the sky and a full moon emerged roundly from behind a sheltering cloud. This was the cue for which the assembly had waited. A cat loves nothing so dearly as a full moon although it gives his presence away. Under the influence of the moonlight all the cats started to sing. In the distance a dog barked his irritation but the cats sang louder, relishing every nuance of their age-old songs.

One piebald tom emerged from the group with his tail cocked in the air. At first I was certain he must be the choirmaster but I sensed, after a while, a note of possessiveness in his tone and a touch of aggressiveness in his stance. He stuck out his chest and snorted. He was, in effect, challenging all-comers to dispute his claims over the she-cat. There were bigger cats in the assembly and for a minute I thought he was going to get away with it. I was particularly surprised when he was ignored by all, especially the lady-cat. Then it dawned on me that this was the neighbourhood clown and that nobody ever took any notice of him. I recognised him as the property of a butcher further down the street. I had a nodding acquaintance with him for I had often surprised him while skulking in my backyard. The other cats obviously enjoyed him for I noticed that some of the more respectable fellows shook their heads at his folly while others threw their lighted eyes heavenwards apologising to the moon for his idiotic behaviour.

Then a large black cat emerged from the males and immediately the piebald entertainer skedaddled to the furthest end of the shed. The black cat was a handsome scoundrel and he knew it. He sang a shrill love-song to the she but before he could deliver himself of an unsolicited encore he was attacked by two other cats. A hysterical free-for-all broke out while the she-cat crooned happily in the background. One crafty cat, of indeterminate age, refused to participate and while the others were at it hammer and tongs he ogled the lady-cat with great skill and experience. He was a romantic-looking chap with several scars on his back and fore-head.

The shrieking of the others was now at its climax. The crafty one arched his back, cocked his tail and manfully strutted to the end of the shed. He turned once and beckoned the she-cat to follow. She did so, rather coyly I thought and both disappeared.

When the free-for-all finished the others saw that they had been cheated and to console themselves they all sang what I concluded to be the most touching refrain of the night. When the song was done they politely bade each other good-night and went their separate ways as silently as they had come.

SKINLESS SAUSAGES

It is a long time now since the first skinless sausage made its appearance on the counters of grocers, pork butchers and other vendors of pork products. Personally speaking it is the most of twenty years since I came face to face with my first skinless sausage. The exact number of years escapes me but I was not unprepared because I had been inured to them by an unusually heavy publicity campaign in the press and on radio. Consequently when I first saw one I was not as shocked as I might otherwise have been.

It happened, of all places, in the charming town of Nenagh. We were, to the best of my recollection, returning from a football game in Dublin and we decided not to break our fast till we arrived in the town of Nenagh at a distinguished hostelry where a warm welcome always awaits the traveller.

First we went to the bar where we called for drinks and where one of our company, more adventurous and more courageous than the rest of us, asked in the calmest manner possible if we might be permitted to inspect the menu.

We were duly presented with same and being fellows with simple tastes, at the time, we opted unanimously for mixed grills.

I have always been intrigued by the composition of mixed grills and in this respect no two hotels are the same. The classic mixed grill consists of morsels of black and white pudding, a chop, a rasher, a brace of sausages, a single pig's kidney and to add colour and gaiety, the half of a moderately-sized tomato fried or raw, according to the disposition of the chef.

There are establishments where more than one chop is given but where this happens it is more than likely that there will be no kidney. Other dining halls fill up the plate with anything handy and often neglect to include the chop which item is considered to be the base of all mixed grills. Others frown upon the inclusion of tomatoes and I have seen mixed grills where one and often two fried eggs usurped the function of the rasher.

Since this, however, is not a dissertation on mixed grills but a treatise having to do in a small way with the first appearance of the skinless sausage, I will say no more about the whimsical and varying compositions of the former.

As we sat in the bar waiting to be called to our meal and sipping our several drops of porter the conversation was relaxed and uncomplicated. The barmaids smiled attractively whenever we looked their way and all in all it could be said that the stage was set for a most entertaining meal.

Eventually we were summoned to the dining room and there we were shown to a table which was set for our exact number. We sat down and soon two wait-resses arrived bearing our several mixed grills with consummate ease in skilled hands. They placed them before us and inquired if we would care for chips. We agreed that they might compliment the meal and ordered some. It was then that we noticed something amiss with the sausages. As I said earlier I was some-what prepared for the phenomena.

The others were caught by surprise but none seemed willing to be the first to speak. One fellow cut a portion of his chop as if there were nothing the matter. Suddenly the youngest member of the party spoke up.

'Hi', he said, 'someone is after whipping the skin off my sausages'. In spite of having said this he promptly devoured the half of one of them and thrust his fork in the other half indicating that it was for the same destination as the first.

Then another member of the company thrust a fork in the larger of his two sausages. He held the sausage aloft for all to see.

'Did you ever see anything as bare in your life', he said and without waiting for confirmation of his observation he immediately thrust the whole sausage into his mouth. One of our party, however, was somewhat of a moralist. He looked at the sausages and a look of disgust appeared on his face.

'They're naked', he shouted. 'Take them away'.

'Certainly', said the fellow who had eaten his sausages whole.

These few comments of mine I hope will be of some help to the student. They are no more than the sum of the reactions of a few to a novelty in its own time but as I say, they may be of some value.

UNKNOWN SPRINTERS

Not long ago in the city of Limerick I saw a man perform an astonishing feat. He was small and extremely fat, and he struck me as a man who wouldn't turn his back on a pound of boiling beef.

In athletic parlance one could say he was out of condition but in cattlemarket terms he might be described as prime. He wore a black, belted overcoat and a hat. One minute he was standing still and the next he was moving like an Olympic sprinter. I have never seen anybody move quite so fast.

In addition his course was neither straight nor true for he had to avoid pedestrians and other obstacles. He reminded me of a trout who has been marooned in a shallow pool. He dodged and darted all over the place but still he covered the ground at a fantastic rate.

Quite suddenly he stopped, all out of breath and with a defeated look on his now perspiring face. Curiosity got the better of me and I threw him sympathetic glance in the hope that he could offer an explanation. He blurted out his story.

Nine years before he had secured a second cousin of his for a bicycle. The cousin had pulled out together with the bicycle and left our friend to pay the piper. 'That was him!' said the fat man. 'I swear that was him I saw driving that yellow car'.

I told him he shouldn't despair; that the incident had served to expose a hidden capacity for short bullet-like bursts of speed. Funnily enough he took little comfort from the fact.

'I am acquainted with younger men than you', I told him, 'who are thin and tall but who could not hold a candle to you in the sort of short sprint you have just accomplished'.

He refused to be consoled and went about his business despondently. But if our fat friend was quick off his mark I know others who are even quicker. These do not come under the public gaze and are never seen in sports stadiums either as competitors or spectators.

In a sense they are the greatest athletes of all because they perform without running shoes or togs and never expect applause. I will give a typical example.

It is a fair day in a small town and suddenly down the centre of the road charges a wild-eyed heifer. The animal in question is the product of a mountainy farm. She has known only the company of hares and elusive snipe and she revolts at her new surroundings. She travels like the wind itself, looking wildly around for any avenue of escape. Her feet slither and her tail is cocked high in the air but there is no diverting her.

Now comes the most amazing sight of all. But let me classify the phenomenon. He is in his fifties, probably sixties, with a grey thatch which is held down by an old brown cap. He wears a heavy overcoat and hobnailed boots. He carries an ashplant in his hand and he wears a gansey with a zip from midriff to Adam's apple. His eyes are glazed but not from drink and there is white spume at the corners of his mouth.

You would expect a man so burdened by apparel and age to be stationary or at most to move at a leisurely walk. This man, however moves like light and because of this nobody takes any notice of him. He dodges bicycles, motors, and ass-and-cars with a liquid fluency of movement and he shouts after the giddy heifer like a man demented.

I see sprinters of this standard at least once a week. A normal man would collapse if he were to undergo such a trial but not our friend. The heifer takes a short turn unexpectedly as heifers are wont to do and it is here our friend fails for he is a straight runner. In negotiating the turn without changing gears he slips and swings off a parked motorcar to save himself from serious damage. But he has enough wind left in him to roar to all and sundry: 'Stop her! She's a bull!'

From his take-off to the time he encountered the turn he must have covered eighty yards. A stopwatch would have shown what I have long believed — that men like him are in world class. Alas, they only run when they have to. But it proves, doesn't it, that there is no shortage of talented sprinters in the country if we care to look for them.

REFERENCES

There is nothing as tricky as writing a reference or being asked to write a reference and last Thursday when a man came to see me on what he termed a matter of grave importance I knew I was once again faced with the same dilemma.

'I want you', he said, 'to ketch a hoult of your pen and make out a reference for my daughter'.

'I don't know you', I said 'and I don't know your daughter'.

'I know', he said, 'but I hear great accounts of you as a writer'.

The writing of references was once the dubious pre-rogative of priests and schoolmasters and it was necessary to be the possessor of a good one from both if one wanted to get a job as a domestic, a clerk, or a civil servant. References were never needed for agricultural or County Council workers. This, I daresay, was because they were paid so little that the best reference they could possibly own was a willingness to work from dawn till dark on as little food and pay as possible. In fact, if a farmer's boy could be found who ate nothing at all, his stomach would be his reference.

But I digress! Where was I, anyway?

Yes! I have in my time come across some unusual references and one in particular comes to mind which was a priceless piece of forgery and a work of art in its own way. It was given to me by a young man who wanted it to begin a career as a barman. It was written on the back of a ballad and it contained the following: *'Behold I am with you all days even unto the consummation of the world'*, and it was signed *'Matthew'*.

'But', I told him, 'this is of no use to you as a reference!'

'That's a shame', he said, 'after I spending the most of an hour taking it down'.

'Where did you get it?' I asked.

'I got it', he said, 'from a tombstone above at the bottom of the churchyard, for' he went on, 'there's always some good written on top about the man that's underneath'.

All he wanted me to do was to add another bit on to it as he considered it too short. 'You can leave the man's name that wrote it at the bottom', he said.

'Fair enough!' I said and I played Paul to his Matthew. *'Take a little wine for thy stomach's sake'*, I wrote, *'and for thy frequent infirmities'*.

'There's no Christian', he said finally, 'would turn down a man with a reference like this!'

The first reference I ever got was from one of my old National teachers. It was a good one and I still have it. The second was more difficult. I was obliged to get one from the Canon of the time, now deceased, God rest him! I went to the presbytery door after Mass and asked the housekeeper if I might see him.

'You came at a bad time', she said, 'but I'll call him out anyway'.

He came out, gave one scathing look at me, and then suddenly inquired: 'How long since your last confession?'

I told him and then he asked with a twinkle in his eye: 'Is the girl from the parish?'

I had great difficulty in persuading him that I didn't want to get married. I was thirteen years of age at the

108

time. He took me into his study and wrote out the reference. He handed it to me and said: 'Don't leave it go too long. A fellow like you would want to be settling down and have someone to look after you'.

Times have changed, however, and letters of reference no longer have a significant influence. The tendancy these days is to suggest the name of a referee who may be contacted to give an account and description of the candidate or applicant. Gone forever are the happy days when the letter began: *'I have known this boy all his life . . .'* and went on to eulogise the subject, ending on a note of such supreme confidence in the person in question that the candidate sounded more like a candidate for canonisation than for a clerkship.

These old-time references were just too good to be true with their abundance of colourful adjectives. There were fine descriptive passages too, like

> of sober and temperate habits, of ingenious and industrious outlook, of outstanding honesty and integrity, possesses a brilliant future and will be of inestimable assistance to anybody who is fortunate enough to secure his services.

THE BIG TEAPOT

I remember a large, nutbrown, earthenware teapot with a bright blue ring around its belly to distinguish it from the kettle. It was so overgrown that it was bigger than what I will call the average kettle. It had a long, happy and most useful life and it held upwards of thirty-two cups of tea. It was used only on occasions of importance such as the day the turf was brought home or the night the aunt came back from America.

It was given out on loan to people who held card gambles and wren-dances. No Station in the parish was complete without it and it was much admired by Canons and curates who declared that it was the biggest and brightest teapot they had ever come across.

When it wasn't being put to the use for which it was originally designed it became a repository for reels of black and white cotton thread, balls of yarn, moth balls, rent notices, Post Office books, and knobs of rustling garlic.

The tea which came out was richer, browner, and tastier, or so it seemed, than that which came out of the average teapot. It had a spout as long as a heron's neck and when the woman of the house poured from it, she was obliged to stand back a few paces lest the stream of golden liquid overshoot its mark and scald an innocent person at the opposite side of the table.

When it appeared to be empty it was then that it revealed its true colours for somehow there was always a cup, or sometimes two cups, left in the bottom.

Then, one night, it was borrowed for an American wake in Knockathea and misfortune befell it. In the heat of the proceedings a young woman who wasn't long married mistook it for a kettle. She filled it with spring water and placed it on top of a roaring fire.

For a while, as the water started to simmer, it seemed as if it would survive the ordeal but as the flames got down to their deadly work there was a small crack inaudible to most of those present. An old woman, however, who was wise in the ways of teapots, cocked her head and said to a friend: 'I own unto God but I'd swear that crack came from a teapot'.

She rose to investigate but as she neared the fire there were several successive sharper cracks and finally the loudest crack of all which split this venerable teapot into two fair halves. The fire, large and cracklesome as it was, was immediately quenched — a tribute surely to the contents of the bisected pot.

It was returned to its owner the following day with all the despairing cermony that a Knight Hospitaller might evince on returning the body of a brave Crusader. 'Twill be no more good for anything!' the woman of the house complained and she on the verge of tears. 'We'll never see the likes of it again!'.

Years rolled by and the teapots came and went. She never again invested in an outsize teapot for none could replace the one which was destroyed by fire.

Aluminium teapots became the rage and these — fair play to them — were of gigantic proportions. Still, the tea was not the same or so it was claimed by those who remembered the nectar of the big pot.

Then, one starry second night of Listowel Races, the woman of the house and her family were in the market place. Tired of bumpers, swingboats and merry-go-rounds, they stood in a half circle round the stall which housed the wheel-o'-fortune and there, sitting in state above a plethora of cups, saucers and enamel buckets, was a tea pot which resembled in all respects the teapot which gave up its life in Knockathea.

There was the same blue ring around its waist and the same contemptuous stance which gave the impression that it belonged in better company. All that was missing was a glowing ring of red coals to warm its bottom and a cargo of drawn tea to enrich its interior.

The man in command of the wheel gave a shout: 'The last four is for sale now!' he said. This was all part of the act for everybody knew that this was only the first four. He went round the ring of investors calling out. 'The last two now missus', or 'the last and only one, sir!'.

Tickets were threepence each and the woman who sought the bluebanded teapot bought the most but allowed her children and husband to buy the rest. The wheel was spun and with a clickety-clickety-clack the arrow passed the number after number until it looked as if it would never stop. Then, slowly but surely, it came to a halt.

'Number one hundred and forty three!' the man shouted. 'Number one four three come forward and take your pick'.

Sure enough, it was the woman of the house who possessed the winning ticket. She raised her hand aloft whilst the members of her family restrained her lest she fall across the palisade.

'What's your choice, missus?' asked the stallholder.

'I'll take the big teapot, if you please, sir', she said.

I'd sooner nor my own departed mother you took anything else, missus', the stallholder told her.

'Come on', she said, ' 'twas won fair and square!'

112

'Take a bucket, ma'am, or a set of ware?'

'Give me out the teapot', she demanded.

'I will, missus, to be sure', she said, 'but the cover is missing and that's why I'm slow about giving it to you'.

'The cover! The cover!' everybody cried in consternation.

But the depression was short-lived. The woman of the house emitted a shout of delight.

'Give it out!' she said in triumph. 'I have the helmet of his dead brother from the night he was broken in Knockathea!'

CRUBEENS

You can send a transatlantic message to a maiden aunt in New Jersey in a matter of seconds but it can take a lifetime to send a simple truth through a quarter-inch of human skull.

The fact remains that if a man nourishes an irrational dislike for a certain commodity, he cannot be converted and all the persuasion in the world will not melt his prejudice nor diminish in any respect the hatred which clings to his partiality.

It is a well-known fact that you will not find a single crubeen for sale in Hyderabad, Timbuctoo, or Calcutta, whereas they are as plentiful as piped water in Tubberneering and Newcastlewest. We have imposed our concepts of culture all over the Eastern hemisphere but we are guilty of neglect and lack of consideration for not having once invited a single black man to join us in debate over a gallon of porter and a quarter-stone of crubeens.

If there is the faintest suggestion that I have something against tapioca or vegetable salad let me say here and now that nothing could be further from the truth but at the same time if someone is going to take the crubeen out of my mouth I'll be hanged if I'm going to stand for it. If someone suggests that they should be eaten in out-of-the-way places by men with corduroy trousers and caps on the sides of their heads let him air his grievance openly in the presence of witnesses and the least he can expect from me is a solicitor's letter in his morning's post.

There is a clique, a sect, a saboteuring segment of our community who think it fashionable to look down their noses at crubeens, who shudder pretentiously at the thought of taking a pig's foot in their dainty hands and eating it with the relish that should be accorded to all delicacies of standing. The same type of people are the ones who wouldn't dream of tapping their feet when a fife and drum band is passing, who would be ashamed of their lives to converse with an old woman who wore a shawl, who walk up the parish church as if they owned it and who worry from morning till night about the impression they make on their betters. Their stomachs are out of tune because they have sold a mighty heritage for frivolities like stuffed tomatoes and mandarin oranges. They have gone from us, for good and glory, to a world that has no room for potato cakes and Bendigo tobacco.

All this is very fine but the dieticians are bound to ask if the crubeen has the requisite number of calories. I doubt very much if there is machinery enough in all the laboratories of the world to analyse accurately the calorific content of a single crubeen because it harbours nourishment and energy which scientists never even dreamed of and I have the assurance of an old woman in Athea who reared forty-two grandchildren that there are more unknown vitamins in a plate of crubeens than you'd find in two creamery tanks full of cod liver oil.

In addition to all this, if we are to place any credence in old wives' tales, crubeens are known to have cured warts, blackheads and goose-pimples and there is complete documentary proof available to support the belief that freshly-boiled crubeens are the bane of ingrown toenails and in seven point four cases out of ten have completely eradicated viciousness and contrariness in cantankerous mothers-in-law.

Crubeens are, above all, the supreme test of friendship even if they do not belong in the vocabularies of head-waiters. The surest way of testing a man's loyalty is to take him into the cocktail bar of a Grade A hotel. When he calls and has paid for the score — that is the time to put your hand into your overcoat pocket and take the crubeen out of its paper bag. If he excuses himself and hurries away to a pressing appointment you know, without doubt, that he is not the kind of man who will keep his head in an emergency and certainly not the sort of neighbour you would call in if the kitchen sink was blocked. But the man who looks at you in admiration and asks you to give him a mouthful is a friend indeed and may be trusted with anything from papering the landing to cutting your corns.

Fortunately for those of us who are diehards there is the assurance that while we have men with smudges on their waistcoats and charity in their hearts the crubeen will occupy a place of honour whenever men gather to celebrate a victory or drown their sorrows over a defeat.

Let those who have a fancy for such things carry stuffed chickens and banana sandwiches to football finals but if you're stuck with a puncture on the road home a man with a crubeen in his mouth is a far likelier proposition.

Faith without good works is dead but it can never be said that crubeens without porter lose any of their attraction. These days we hear much of the better way of life. My advice to those who would improve their situation is to journey afar to fair-grounds and foreign publichouses. After arrival at the chosen spot they should look carefully about them and upon seeing the bones of crubeens scattered at their feet should pause, sniff and take up the trail, thereby spreading confusion among the ranks of those who are spying on them and following faithfully the tenets and obligations of men who are not ashamed of crubeens.

BAKING A CAKE

All women like to bake buns. Buns call for no great effort and because of their size are quickly baked. Unless I am greatly mistaken there are a number of reliable bun-powders available at reasonable prices. A good spatter of water is all that is required to produce a reliable batter. All women too are useful pancake makers but not all are useful cake-makers or even moderately-good cake-makers.

This is why I feel constrained to take the matter up immediately. As one grows older one feels a greater sense of civic responsibility. I have long felt that the making of buns and apple pies do the same thing for a woman that a hair-do does, not a major hair-do but a minor one. There is no great risk involved in a hair-set just as there is no great risk involved in the making of buns, apple pies, pancakes, etcetera.

There is a risk, however, in submitting oneself to a complete permanent wave. It is a huge undertaking and fewer women go in for the permanent wave these days. If it goes wrong there is nothing one can do about it afterwards, apart from having a good cry. Tears, we are told, are good for the complexion but this is poor consolation to a woman who has spent up to fifty shillings and the better part of a day in a hairdressing establishment. No, the risk is too great and the set is the easier and the cheaper way out.

The same applies to the making of cakes. The cake is a big undertaking and few are willing to risk it because so many things can go wrong. As a youngster I was once witness to a terrible tragedy in this respect of cake-making.

I cannot have been more than five years of age at the time. It so happened that a young man in our street got married. She was a very nice girl and it was easy to make friends with her. She often entrusted me with messages. These were small assignments which involved the occasional quarter pound of tea or small tins of beans. She came, after a while, to rely on me and took to confiding in me.

She had great ambitions in the cooking and baking line and she would spend long evenings baking buns and apple pies and other such pleasant trivia for her husband's supper. I was whole-heartedly on her side and was always an interested spectator when she readied the table for a spot of dough-mixing. We were a pretty good team, if I say so myself and considering we had so little experience we turned out some attractive pieces of stuff. We were best at scones and her husband would praise these loudly. She even started to give gifts of them to older housewives in the street. These house-wives, women of vast experience, approved of her efforts and said that she had much promise.

One evening, in fact, I heard my mother say that the young woman's apple pies were as good as her own. This was no small compliment, because remember my mother had twenty years front-line experience behind her.

There were other compliments too. She bought an ass-rail of turf from a small farmer and when he had deposited it in her backyard she asked him in for a cup of tea. He agreed so she decided to try out some rhubarb pie she had baked the day before. This man was as big a rogue as you would find and probably because he had overcharged her for the turf he was loud in his praise of the rhubarb pie. Said he, 'I've eaten a heap of pies in my day but the pie I've et now whacks the daylight out of the lot of them'.

When he saw how pleased the young housewife was he went further: 'I've eaten in hotels', he said, 'and I've eaten at wakes and weddings but I declare to God I've never put the likes of this pie inside my shirt before'.

After he had departed I was given a piece of the pie and she watched me closely while I ate it.

'Well', she asked when I had finished.

' 'Tis as nice as I ever ate', I said not altogether truthfully. The pie was nice enough but there were several women in the street who could have done a better job with their eyes closed. When her husband came from work he praised the pie too but then he was in the habit of praising everything about her. This, of course, is not an unnatural thing in young husbands and it is only what one would expect of them. He often told her things which were not even remotely true, such as she was the most beautiful girl in the world and nicer than any film star. To tell the truth she was not a bad-looking girl but she was no film star.

All the compliments which were showered on her rhubarb pie did her more harm than good. She would sit, often for ten minutes at a time, in deep thought and when I would ask her if she wanted any messages done she would look at me absently. This went on for weeks and it was plain that she was trying to resolve something within herself.

Suddenly one evening she leaped from the chair where she had been sitting and made the following announcement:

'You know what I'm going to do?' she said and her

eyes glowed when she said it, 'I am going to bake a cake'.

I was delighted because I knew that my help would be needed. The date fixed for the actual baking was the following day. That night I mentioned to my mother that Mrs. So-and-So was going to bake a cake.

'What kind of cake?' my mother asked.

'A cherry cake', I said.

My mother shook her head thoughtfully, 'there is more in the making of a cherry cake', she said, 'than meets the eye, still', she went on, 'we all have to start sometime'.

The following day I presented myself at the young woman's house and we started work without delay. I was allowed to beat up the eggs and I can safely say that no eggs ever got a better beating.

We got our cake tin ready and we smoothed out our butter paper. We then transferred the mixture to the tin. We opened the oven door and without more ado we put in the cake. Then we waited and we opened the oven door after a specified period to see if all was going well. When the door was opened I was told to be on the look-out for draughts. No draughts got in. I'm certain of that.

The oven door was closed again and we waited. Finally the time came to take out the cake. The oven door was opened and then with a cloth to protect her hands she gently lifted the tin from the oven.

The cake looked good but it had to be given a chance to cool off. She stood nearby like a Polynesian spear-fisherman with a long knife in her hand. The time had come. With two deft strokes she cut a slice from the cake. We almost dared not look. But we had to look and what we saw was that every last cherry had sunk to the bottom.

She sat down, buried her head in her hands and cried. I stood helplessly by. After a while she rose and shook herself. She was made of good stuff.

'We'll give this to the hens', she announced, 'and we'll try again tomorrow'.

FEMALE PAINTERS

I have long admired the professional decorator

The expertise with which he prepares his walls, doors and windows appeals to my artistic sense. It is, however, when his blowlamp sends its searing breath across wastelands of old paint that I become really involved. As he scrapes away the blistering mess I am reminded of springtime.

Odd, you may say, that it should remind me of springtime. It does, however, put me in mind of the spring sun melting the winter snow from green fields, readying them, as it were, for the glorious paint-brush of Spring.

But enough of this!

The subject of to-day's investigation is not the professional but rather the female painter.

Here is no carefully laid-out plan, no readying of surfaces or scraping of paint. Here is all-out attack from the beginning to the end of the campaign. Women painters are hard to identify. The professional wears his white coat as if he were born in it and his procedure in public is sedate and composed. He knows he is a painter and those who know him know he is a painter. On the other hand the female could be a character out of a pantomime. Around her head a towel is wrapped tightly like a turban and around her body is buttoned and pinned the oldest of old coats. Take the brush from her hand and I defy you to find out what her vocation is. You will probably hazard a guess that she is an entry in a fancy-dress competition.

Put a brush in her hand, however, and a pot of

paint by her side and there is no mistaking her bent. She is a ferocious painter. That is to say she paints everything that comes in her way from door-knobs to light-switches. I knew a woman who painted electric light bulbs. They will cover more ground in an hour than a professional will in a day. It is only when the job of painting is done that their work really begins for, while the professional's job is completed with the last stroke, the woman's is only halfway through. She has to go over certain parts again for it is not until she has finished the first round that she stands back to survey her handiwork. Having completed the second round there is now the business of mopping up. First of all there are the hundreds of old newspapers with which she has covered the floor at the outset. These must be bundled together and burned under personal supervision. Then the floor must be washed with turpentine and afterwards with soap and water. Hands have to be washed and this is no easy job for while she may not have the knack of distributing paint evenly she certainly has the knack of accumulating it. When the hands are satisfactorily cleaned of paint she unwinds the turban and tosses her head to left and right. Her hair bobs jerkily at first, freed from its long confinement. She ruffles it with paint-free fingers and loosens it so that it regains some of its earlier brilliance.

Then she heaves a great sigh for her labours are nearing their end. She unbuttons and unpins the old coat. This is a safe time for other members of the family to return to the household. Whether it is good, bad, or indifferent, the work must be admired; otherwise severe and lasting friction may be the outcome. Always insist that it would have been much more expensive to hire a professional painter. In fact this might be a good time to run down all tradesmen and professionals. Don't overdo it, though, or she will know you are only laying it on. Do not suggest that she should get her hair done. She will suggest this herself the following morning. It would never do to associate the doing of her hair with the spreading of the paint. Her intent was to do a fast and cheap job so that the hair-do might quite rightfully be regarded as an extra expense.

One thing which intrigues me about painting done by women is the time it takes to dry. For days, and often for weeks, afterwards, one picks up the odd streak on coat and trousers. It may look dry and feel dry but it has the unhappy art of attaching itself to the clothes especially when one is wearing one's best suit. It never attaches itself to the women themselves — only to husbands and visitors.

Be all that as it may, I like women-painters. There is a great bustle to them and great courage in their approach. The job is never really done, of course, for while there is a spot of paint left in the house they will be going about at the most unexpected times touching up weak spots and searching, often in vain, for ways to use up the remaining paint. No door, window or chest is safe while women painters are in this mood. They love to touch up legs of tables so that there is always a surprise waiting for the man who sits down to his meals. They do not believe in *Wet Paint* signs. I once taxed my own spouse with this and she insisted that the paint was not wet, only sticky or greasy. When I showed her the paint on my clothes she insisted I was deliberately leaning against painted places.

The reason I write about women painters is because April is their busy month and any day now yours will appear with a brush in her hand, a turban on her head, and the eager look of a small girl on her face.

HAIR-OIL

It is many a long day now since I invested in my first fourpenny bottle of hair-oil.

The coif obtained by tap-water was of short duration and there was no smell from it.

The fourpenny bottles came in cards. They were long and narrow and all that was written on the label was 'High Quality Brilliantine'. But the cards were far more descriptive and if one cared to examine the small print there was much to be learned. For instance, although you would never guess it from looking at the bottle, the oil within contained a secret ingredient which was guaranteed 'to preserve the natural quality of the hair'. There was a drawing of a polished-looking scoundrel whose face held a naive cunning but whose hair was plastered to his head without a rib out of place.

These fourpenny bottles are a thing of the past and a new range of oils and creams have taken their place. If you were to ask a shopkeeper to-morrow for a four-penny bottle of hair-oil he would probably laugh at you and tell the story, with embellishments, to his wife that night. The demand now is for medically-guaranteed liquids and solids which contain natural hair-foods.

Hair-food has always intrigued me and it was a smart man who first thought it up. What exactly is hair-food and how does one get it through the skin of the scalp. Some heads I know are so thick that the food would have to be despatched through the ears if contact is to be made with the roots, while other heads are so thin-skinned that the brains, if any, might be in danger of food-poisoning.

But hair-food is not to be laughed off and there may be something to it after all. Hair-oil, to-day, comes in bottles as in the past but nowadays the bottles are carefully covered by colourful cardboard containers and leaflets as informative and instructive as a chapter from a medical text-book. These leaflets will assure you that this new specially-processed oil contains ingredients which restore the hair to its natural colour and which also satisfies hungry hair. Hungry hair is a serious matter and one may presume that hungry hair is the chief cause of baldness because if a hair is hungry enough it is likely to revert to cannibalism and start eating its neighbours.

Other oils, mostly imported, are alive with vitamins which 'keep your hair happy' and 'give longer life to ageing hair'.

I remember a time when rainwater was regarded as the most reliable of hair tonics. This was widely known as 'duck's hair-oil' and was perhaps the most popular and plentiful of old-time hair remedies but I personally prefer to remember the innocent face of a young fellow at his first dance. The contents of a fourpenny bottle of hair-oil were poured over his head before he set out and when the half-sets were under way rivulets of oil ran down his face and under his collar but he showed no discomfort and when the dance was over he retired to the back of the hall and withdrew a comb from his back-pocket. He didn't comb his hair. He racked it and he kept on racking it until the music started again.

Fourpenny bottles of hair-oil came in a variety of colours. There were yellow and green and blue among others but the yellow was reputed to be more genuine than any and you couldn't convince a man who used yellow hair-oil that green or blue was just as good.

Many people have never used hair oil and there are still some who insist that it is a sign of feminity, hooliganism, perjury, instability, or stupidity but in spite of this when dry weather comes a man needs more than water to keep his hair down. An old man I know, who lives in the country, is violently anti-hair-oil. When he reads of rowdyism or bank robberies he will tell you that it is the work of 'bucks with hair-oil and tie-pins'. A landlady with whom I once lodged would allow no hair-oil on the premises. She couldn't get it out of her pillow-slips and it contaminated other innocent garments in the wash.

Men who use large quantities of hair-oil will have the reputation of being slippery and oily and we often hear terms like: 'He's oily, that fellow!' or: 'He's a slippery knacker!' whereas the persons in question may be upright citizens whose only weakness is a liking for a drop of hair-oil.

Hair-oil is certainly the answer to wayward hair and it is a known fact that careful application of paraffin oil is the scourge of colonist fleas, louse-eggs, and other unwelcome vermin who would populate man's unprotected pate.

THE FAMILY HISTORY

When I was younger I was friendly with a man who promised himself that one day he would write a history of his own family. There were more famous families and more illustrious families in the locality and it was felt that he would be better rewarded if he wrote about these. But no. All he wanted to do was write about his own. He told a local schoolmaster what he was about and asked him if he would be good enough to look over the history when it was written. The teacher agreed but then he addressed himself to the would-be historian as follows:

'Do not go back too far', he said. 'You are on the crest of a wave now and it would seem that such was always the case amongst the past members of your family. Maybe it was but I know that in my own case I would never write a history of my family for the good reason that, unlike you, I know too much about them'.

The historian, however, was determined to press ahead. Other sane and sober elders in the community advised him against it. One old man asked him why he wanted to write about his own family rather than another family in the first place.

'Because', said the would-be historian, 'they are my own'.

'So are mine', said the elder, 'but you'll never catch me writing about them'.

This did not deter the historian. He was in possession

of relatively ample means so he went about asking others if they remembered such an uncle or such an aunt, such a great-uncle or such a great-aunt and so round turned out to be possessed of limitless information he required was slow in coming in. He sat down one night and gave the matter his most careful consideration. Think as he did he came no nearer to a solution. He rose and there and then decided to go to a pub where liquid inspiration was always readily available.

The pub, he discovered, was a mine of information. Its occupants who were eager and willing to join company with anyone who would include them in a round turned out to be possessed of limitless information about the historian's family.

Not a bad word would they say against them and they assured him that anybody who did was a thorough blackguard. Never, they declared, in the history of mankind was there such a family for honesty, bravery, good looks, dignity, and true humility. The more they drank the more fanciful their stories became. Some even wept at the injustice of a world which, did not canonize such antecedents as the historian's. That there were no counts, knights or princes in his background was an enormous affront to honest labours and selfless suffering.

All the old arguments against the writing of the history were frittering away and he could see now that it was jealousy that prompted the objections. The drink flowed freely as they discussed the humorous side of the family. Then came the charitable side of the family. Then came the warlike side and it emerged slowly but emphatically that all the members of all the branches were truly what one might call 'men for all seasons'.

Happily our friend went homeward but if he awoke

in the morning with a sick head and a reduction in the size of his purse he also awoke with the knowledge that he would be quite justified in starting the book. He purchased jotters and pencils and at the same hour on the following night he proudly wended his way to the pub. He went around requesting the patrons to repeat the statements they had made the night before but all refused to do so. Our friend was astonished. Was it how they had led him up the garden path or was it that they had merely indulged him because of the free drinks? They assured him that this was not the case, that they were simple, unlettered men who did not want their names in the papers, not to mention books. They begged to be excused. He tried to cajole them with drinks and went so far as to offer them money but they were adamant. What they should have told him was that in the long run all families get their share. No one stays for too long at the top and it is a wise man who is content with his lot, provided it is a reasonable one.

In the histories of all families there is a faulty bulb for every shining light. For every distinguished member there are scores of ordinary ones in addition to normal quota of ruffians and scoundrels.

As an elder in the community once said to me: 'A family is a fine thing so long as it is somebody else's'.

CORNER BOYS

I have nothing against corner-boys so long as they have nothing against me and, indeed, those who stand at corners on Sundays and half-days are not, in the strict sense, corner-boys at all. They don't look like corner-boys and to the trained eye it is obvious that their tenure is accidental and brief. They look like amateurs and their posture is a far cry from that of the professional who is immune to hail, rain or shine.

The dedicated corner-boy can stand in the same position for an hour at a time. He may twitch a facial muscle or adjust a shoulder blade but these moves are not visible to the naked eye. His eyes move consistently and nothing is overlooked from the strut of the alert crow, who has come to the street for his lunch, to the number and appointment of all the television aerials within his ken. The black lines under his eyes, so easily mistaken for lechery and debauch are, in reality, eye muscles. These eye muscles are highly developed and in the majority of ordinary people they do not exist at all. When the eye is the only part of the body operating it is only natural that it should be the most potent. You may ask if this form of eye-work is as demanding as other forms of labour such as ploughing and breaking stones. There is every reason to believe that it is. The common or garden corner-boy has a phenomenal appetite and he is not an early riser. He looks tired and is rarely fitted for any other type of work. He is a heavy sleeper and does not wake easily when contingency arises. There can, therefore, be little doubt that his trade is as exhausting as any other.

When he takes a break, at dinner and supper times, his movements are slow and deliberate. He plods homeward cow-like.

He is not excitable for I myself have seen his reaction to incidents which have often caused excitement and upheaval in others.

If a well-to-do tourist pulls up his sports-car and looks for directions he lazily takes a hand from his trousers pocket and, without opening his mouth, re-directs the errant motorist with his thumb. Others—not corner-boys—I have seen who have become almost obstreperous, who have thrust their heads inside car-windows and spent minutes over unnecessary details.

When the professional corner-boy moves it is a movement of the least demanding kind. It is wholly natural and not in the least studied, except for short periods immediately after lunch and breakfast. Then he goes all-out— as if he were afraid of being dismissed as if his life depended upon it. He should have no such fears and, to tell the truth, he really hasn't. His fear is that something will happen while he is away. Such is the speed of his return that he is inclined to bump into people and take chances while crossing roads. You may ask why he should cross roads, why he should by-pass more accessible corners to arrive at a corner which is out of the way? He does it for the same reason as every commuter, because the corners near home do not offer the same advantages.

But let me return to what is likely to happen while he is away from the corner. Somebody might fall from a bicycle or somebody might get a parking ticket. There is always the possibility on an interesting dog-fight and the added spectacle when a civic-spirited passer-by gets attacked while trying to intervene. A child may fall on his face and cause an unholy din, or an adventurous cat make a sudden sortie from one door to another. These are but a few of the things which can and do happen. During storms a slate can miss a passer-by by inches or, when the roads are icy, a car may skid. I have detected the faintest of sly smiles on the faces of corner-boys on occasions like these. If there is an accident his movements are cheetah-like and automatic. The speed at which he negotiates the other side of the corner makes the onlooker want to believe that he hasn't moved at all—that he has been standing at the other side all the time.

Are we to believe then that he is anti-social; that he shrinks from the onerous responsibility of the eye-witness? Let us be fair! His dodge is motivated by the belief that, if he did not volunteer to be a witness, nobody would believe him in the first place.

He is legally entitled to stand at every and any corner of his choosing with the exception of the extremely busy corner where he is liable to be buffeted too often by inconsiderate passers-by. Naturally, this is annoying and accounts for the absence of corner-boys from the major streets of cities.

Weather is no obstacle except in extreme cold when he hunches himself up. His movements are as economical as always and one wonders at his durability and hardihood. One bitterly cold day, with driving winds and frequent sleet, I looked out of my window on several occasions over a period of several hours. There was nobody out of doors with the exception of one corner-boy, one cloaked postman and two policemen. Our friend will have the hell of a cold tomorrow, I thought but when tomorrow came it was I who had the cold and our friend was still at his corner—and serve me right—for his antics were none of my business in the first place.

POTATO-CAKES

Lest there be any doubt about it let me make it clear that nobody has bribed me to take up the pen in praise of potato-cakes.

I do so because, not so long ago, I came across two marriageable girls who had never heard of potato-cakes. They were authorities on rum omelette and loganberry jelly. One had devised an original recipe for meringue crumb pudding and the other blandly announced that her Polish tarts had taken second prize at a metropolitan agricultural show. Neither showed any contrition for not having heard of potato-cakes. One may draw one's own conclusions but I am of the opinion that the pair are destined to remain unmarried permanently unless they lift themselves out of the lethargy which has made them ignorant of the role of the griddle.

A hot potato-cake is like an Indian Summer. It soothes and refreshes. It has a strong taste which is more than one can say for vegetable dumplings. It may be sliced in two halves so that the steam rises from its interior in a mist of surpassing fragrance. It can be smeared on the inside of both parts with melting butter or it needn't be sliced at all because it is just as attractive with a bit of butter on top of it.

One of the reasons why potato-cakes are so little in evidence at this present time is that they are too easy to make. All that one needs is a griddle or an outsize frying-pan, a little flour and butter and a few left-over potatoes. If the ingredients were difficult to come by and of foreign extraction there would be no scarcity but the surest way to confuse a modern miss is to ask her boil an egg or bake a few potato-cakes.

The perfect potato-cake is not made overnight. Like everything else there must be trial and error even a little heartbreak when the mixture turns out dumpy and damp or lumpy and indigestible but there should be no despondency because of early failures. It took a conscientious woman of my acquaintance several years before she perfected her potato-cakes. Overdoing it a bit, one might say, but not when one considers the nett result. Her husband, an intractable and unpredictable delinquent in the early years of marriage, is now her devoted slave. He, who once had an alcoholic tremor in both hands, is now her corn-parer in chief, her ware-dryer and hair-dryer and, last but not least, an almost insufferable boaster of her inimitable culinary techniques.

Opinion is divided as to whether the child of today can watch television and do his lessons at the same time. The child holds that he can. The parent holds otherwise. There is merit on both sides. A man can cut his finger-nails without taking his eyes from the screen and a woman can do her knitting. I know a bright young man who can read a book and watch television without strain but there is one task which defies them all. You will not eat potato-cakes and watch television at the same time. You will not—because your attention will be wholly focussed on the plate and you will regard with suspicion the least movement of those who share the table. Potato-cakes have a knack of disappearing which deceives the distracted eye and the only way to assure oneself of a full share is to trust nobody until the appetite is sated. Friendship and family loyalty are virtues to which all should aspire but to rely upon the restraints of others when potato-cakes are on the menu is pushing friendship a bit too far and asking too much of loyalty.

I haven't eaten a potato-cake now in six months. Maybe this will serve to remind those whose fault it is. Maybe a certain conscience will be disturbed when left-over spuds are dumped without ceremony into rubbish-cans. Maybe there will be others like myself who, by subtle suggestion and innuendo, will drive the salient point home that six months without potato-cakes is carrying the game a bit too far.

Far-seeing mothers, who are adept at making potato-cakes, should instruct their daughters well. Honours in Algebra is not to be scoffed at but, I ask you, which will pay the better dividend in the long run.—Honours in Algebra or a pass in making potato-cakes? I know, and you know but does the bride of tomorrow know? I am not saying that potato-cakes will resolve all the problems that arise in the early years of marriage but you can be certain that they will go a long way towards eliminating impulsive departures to momma. They may not be the answer to the in-law problem but in-laws tend to become secondary tribulations when the palate is under the influence of potato-cakes.

Cold weather is the best weather for potato-cakes and the best time to eat them is after returning from long walks when the air is brisk and days tend to grow shorter. They are an accredited repast and constitute a full meal in themselves when fortified by butter, especially farmers' butter. They are essentially, as I said, a winter diet because young or early potatoes lack the body that is required.

Potato-cakes do not belong to cliques and this may be the root cause of their non-appearance. But you won't brush them off so easily.

I don't want any potato-cake mixture in packages either nor instant potato-cake in tins. You must use left-over potatoes and not freshly-boiled one. It's logic in itself, isn't it? If there are potatoes left over after the dinner then by all the powers that be a full dinner was not eaten and if a full dinner was not eaten a full tea is imperative and how better can you have a full tea than by having potato-cakes.

DOORS AND HALF-DOORS

It was either 1937 or 1938. I cannot be sure.

I was hurrying to school when a woman hailed me from her doorway.

'Run down quick', she said, 'to So-and-So's and tell him his sister is on the 'phone from America'.

I did as I was bade.

'Knock hard!' she called after me, 'because if you don't he mightn't hear you'.

When I reached the door I knocked hard and waited. No response so I knocked harder. Still no response so I kicked the door until the front of the house seemed to shake.

'Who's there?' a voice called from the inside.

'Your sister is on the 'phone from America!' I called back.

'One second' said the voice, 'till I put on my trousers'.

A moment passed and he emerged in shirt and trousers. There wasn't time for coat or shoes. Together we raced up the street but when we got to the house where the 'phone was the American sister was no longer with us. A scapegoat was needed.

'Why for', he shouted at me, 'did you kick my door?'

That was my thanks!

I hastened to school, vowing it would be a long time before I put a boot to a door again.

Some people hate opening their doors and no amount of knocking will succeed. Like most boys I frequently delivered messages and often it was necessary to pound on a door before being answered.

On Saturdays, by contract, I used to deliver meat for a certain butcher. There was one particular door which had seen sturdier days and which creaked and shuddered when struck by palm or knuckles. It was a door which resented touch of any kind and it was hard to blame it for it had suffered decades of wind and rain. An old couple lived behind it's shivering timbers and they were reluctant to open it. Maybe they were sparing it, trying to get it to last as long as themselves or, more likely, they could not afford the cost of a new one. I always knocked on it very gently or what I believed to be very gently. It always protested and so did its owners.

'Why are you so anxious to try to break down the door?' they would say.

I would point out that I had tipped it several times with my fingers and, getting no redress, had resorted to the knuckles.

'D'you think 'tis made of iron?' the old man would say.

'Is it how you think doors grow on trees?' the old woman would say.

'Why don't you get a knocker?' I would put in.

'And have every young buck in the town hammering it, is it?' said the old man.

'The door would never stand up to it', said the old woman.

The old man would then launch into a long sermon about the way people treated his door. He maintained that people never treated their own doors the way they treated other doors. 'Do unto other doors as you would unto your own' was the gist of his long discourse.

Half-doors are gone forever, routed and overwhelmed

140

by mass-produced excuses. The half-door had no equal. There was no need to knock. You just leaned across it and said, 'God bless all here!' and before you knew it you would be told to come in but to watch the hens as you did.

Hens hated half-doors. Hens are poor and graceless fliers and couldn't fly over them. They might manage to perch on the half-door but here they were exposed to abuse and attack.

Knocking at doors in the middle of the night is a precarious pursuit no matter how justified it might seem. Certain, porter-laden, home-going bucks were fond of kicking doors indiscriminately at all hours of the morning. This was how they got their kicks and they took savage delight in kicking the doors of a dark, deserted street and then running out of reprisal as fast as their legs could carry them.

Yet I do not approve of bells on doors. You press the bell and wait. Sometimes you cannot be sure whether the machinery is in order or not. There is also a total absence of satisfaction. People who have knocked at doors all their lives as a method of gaining entry are confused by doorbells. The habit of knocking is difficult to overcome. Knocking or habitual knocking is as hard to give up as cigarettes or television and I have heard of people who were driven to assault and battery when deprived of it.

Civic Guards and postmen like to knock at doors. Their knocks are distinctive and, while never loud, are designed to be heard in every corner of the house.

Knocking is not confined to humans and my wife, when she was a Miss, had a red setter named 'Watch' who used to knock at the front door with his tail.

During the old licensing laws every pub had its own knock, known only to its customers, to men who could

141

be trusted not to spread the word that an after-hours trade was going on. Civic Guards, if they had wanted to, could easily have imitated such knocks but God bless them they never stooped to it. No, they knocked with the authority vested in them and you always knew when you asked 'Who's out?' that the answer would be: 'Guards on public house duty!'

BY THE SAME AUTHOR

SELF PORTRAIT
John B. Keane's own story has all the humour and insight one would expect, but it has too, the feeling of an Irish country-man for his traditional way of life and his ideals for the Ireland he loves.

38p

THE MAN FROM CLARE
Personal tragedy of an ageing athlete who finds he no longer has the physical strength to maintain his position as captain of the team, and his reputation as the best footballer in Clare.

35p

THE YEAR OF THE HIKER
The "Hiker" is the much hated father who deserted his wife and family twelve years previously and whose return is awaited with fear. This play portrays with tears and laughter the fears and happiness of the Lacey family.

35p

LETTERS OF A SUCCESSFUL T.D.
This bestseller takes a humorous peep at the correspondence of an Irish parliamentary deputy. Keane's eyes have fastened on the human weaknesses of a man who secured power through the ballot box, and uses it to ensure the comfort of his family and friends.

50p

BIG MAGGIE
The theme of this play is the domination of an Irish family by a hard and tyrannical mother, and it brings out all the humour and pathos of Irish rural life.

Hardcover £1.25

LETTERS OF AN IRISH PRIEST
This book follows his best seller *Letters of a Successful T.D.* There is a riot of laughter in every page and its theme is the correspondence between a country parish priest and his nephew who is studying to be a priest. Fr. O Mora has been referred to by one of his parishioners as one who "is suffering from an overdose of racial memory aggravated by religious bigotry". This book gives a picture of a way of life which though in great part is vanishing is still familiar to many of our country-men who still believe "that priests could turn them into goats". It brings out all the humour and pathos of Irish life. It is hilariously funny and will entertain and amuse everybody.

45p

MOLL

"When a presbytery gets a new housekeeper it becomes like a country that gets a change of government, like a regiment that gets a new sergeant-major, or like a family that gets a new stepmother. A new housekeeper is like a new moon and a new moon can bring anything from a tidal wave to an earthquake", says Fr. Brest when Canon Pratt is about to hire their new housekeeper, Miss Mollie Kettle alias "Moll". These are the first forebodings of the calamity that is about to befall them. Is "Moll" "a great woman entirely" or is she "cunning, sharp, deadly, evil personified"? Did a late curate who was in her care die of a mixture of maleficence, malnutrition and pernicious anaemia? "Moll" would work for no less than a canon, for in her own words: "'Tis hard to come back to the plain black and white when one is used to the purple". So "Moll" is hired, established her regime, the canon and parish begin to prosper, the curates suffer. She gets a choir going the church is repaired, a new school is built—yet the curates groan under their share in the household chores, their new duties at the regular bingo sessions ("for the ultimate role of the Catholic Church in Ireland is the propagation of Bingo") and whinge at the rasping screech of the dear housekeeper—"no banshee is her equal".

Hilariously funny, *Moll*, the new comedy by Ireland's most influential and prolific dramatist, will entertain and amuse everybody.

40p

THE FIELD

The Field is a play about the social and moral effects of land greed and the scene is an isolated village in Kerry.

50p

If you would be interested in receiving announcements of forthcoming publications send your name and address to:

THE MERCIER PRESS

4 BRIDGE STREET,

CORK